# SUCCESS IN LIFE.

# THE ARTIST.

BY

MRS. L. C. TUTHILL.

"Heaven and earth, advantages and obstacles, conspire to educate genius."
*Fuseli.*

CINCINNATI: HENRY W. DERBY. | NEW YORK: JAMES C. DERBY.

1854.

DAVID HILLS & CO., STEREOTYPERS,
141 Main Street, Cincinnati.

# CONTENTS.

## INTRODUCTORY CHAPTER.

"One age moves onward, and the next builds up
Cities and gorgeous palaces, where stood
The rude log-huts of those who tamed the wild;
Rearing from out the forests they had felled,
The goodly frame-work of a famous State."—*Lowell.*

In this beautiful world, so bountifully provided with all things for man's use and comfort, it is a painful thought that there are human beings who have not as much skill in Art as the bird or the beaver.

Quite in advance of those miserable creatures who neither build huts for shelter, clothe themselves, nor cook their food, are the savages who construct wigwams, invent instruments of warfare against man and beast, wear clothing, and know the use of fire. A wide step toward civilization is taken, when man builds himself a substantial house, changes cotton, flax, or wool into garments, and invents ways and means to transport himself from place to place, either in the canoe which glides over the waters, or on the back of the fleet horse which he has tamed and domesticated.

Scarcely has he made himself comfortable in these respects, nay, even long before this, the savage models the clay, or shapes the stone into an image from the rude conception in his own mind, and bows before it in dumb adoration; here is the dark dawn of Religion and of Art.

He has, moreover, an instinctive love of the beautiful. Else, why does he paint with brilliant colors his naked body, adorn himself with the gay plumage of birds, and hang about his neck ocean-shells of "purest ray serene?" Delightedly, he gazes at his decorated person in the glassy pool or placid lake. Even in his untutored mind, there is an earnest longing for something beyond the mere gratification of animal appetite.

The "living soul," impressed with the divine image of its Creator, admires and emulates His works. Lord of the "great globe itself," man learns in time to appropriate to its right use, all which he inherits. He renders inanimate matter vocal;—he makes it a visible exponent of his spirituality; he gives it character, expression, beauty—everything but life.

There is a longing of soul, a perpetual seeking for something beyond and above the perishable, the gross and "beggarly elements" of earth,—hence the necessity for the Fine Arts—the Arts which adorn, cheer and elevate this mortal existence.

As man advances in civilization and refinement, the Arts which beautify life keep pace with this advancement. Poetry, music, architecture, sculpture, painting, engraving, landscape gardening, are all developed beneath the fostering care of genius and wealth.

"Art is power. That is the original meaning of the word. It is the creative power by which the soul of man makes itself known through some external manifestation or outward sign." . Poetry and its natural ally, music, are among the loftiest "manifestations" of the soul; but we must here dissever them from the noble fellowship of Art, leaving it for other and abler hands to point out the "success" which has been achieved by poets and musicians. The painter, the sculptor, the architect and the engraver, are the artists whose examples will here be shown as beacon-lights, both to encourage and to warn the young who have received the gift of genius.

In the merchant, the lawyer, and the mechanic, our own age and country furnished the examples of successful effort, but a wider range is taken to illustrate the success of the artist.

The language of Art is universal. The memorials of genius are the rich heritage of every age and every clime. The magic fountain, from which the gifted have ever imbibed inspiration, is not exhausted; nature is still the same bountiful mother, and the soul of man still strives for a closer alliance with its Divine Creator. Our country is ripe for Art. Our painters are already a goodly company. The materials, with which the sculptor and architect are to gain imperishable renown are scattered with luxurious profusion over our wide land, and our artists have made the stones speak, and are eloquent in marble.

But are we taking the lead of all other nations, in the most noble, as well as the most useful of arts, Architecture? * Truth replies, we are not. Are some of our most highly educated and most highly gifted young men earnestly devoting themselves to Art, because they infinitely prefer devotion to that pursuit to eminence in professional life? Are there any philanthropists among us seeking out youthful genius, borne down and almost crushed by poverty, and giving it the needful culture and opportunity? If so, success—to each and all, success.

* Architecture proper, naturally arranges itself under five heads:

*Devotional.*—Including all buildings raised for God's service or honor.

*Memorial.*—Including both monuments and tombs.

*Civil.*—Including every edifice raised by nations or societies, for purposes of common business or pleasure.

*Military.*—Including all buildings for defence.

*Domestic.*—Including every rank and kind of dwelling house.

## CHAPTER II.

### THE CHILDHOOD OF THE ARTIST.

"O child! O new-born denizen
Of life's great city! On thy head
The glory of the morn is shed
Like a celestial benizon."—*Longfellow.*

A GLORIOUS "calling" is that of the Artist. An earnest, genuine, truthful Artist is not to be met on every highroad and every day in the year. Like comets, Artists seem to be out of the common order of things, only astonishing and puzzling the world now and then. A struggle, and fierce contest they too frequently have to maintain, before they can get a standing-place among their fellow-men "What use? What use?" is the cry. "Away with your easel! Dont spoil that nice block of marble!"

Yet the Artist has his lawful place in the world as truly as the comet has in the solar system, and sooner or later, he will find and occupy it nobly.

The aptitude to excel in Art, which we call *genius*, is as truly the gift of God, as is the beauty of the human countenance. The very plays of children indicate the talents with which they have been entrusted.

When the shepherd-boy Giotto* amused himself with draw-

* Giotto, a celebrated Italian painter, born near Florence, A. D. 1276.

ing upon flat stones with a piece of chalk, who was his teacher? Nature. Why should he, more than any other peasant, select one from the flock which he tended and draw its figure upon the flat rock? The painter Cimabue, could answer the question, and he did so; for finding the shepherd-boy thus employed he immediately recognized the hand of genius; he sought Giotto's parents and gained their consent to educate the youthful painter; for even genius must be educated; that is, whatever nature has given, must be drawn forth and perfected.

Michel Angelo,*—the architect, sculptor and painter,—was sent to a grammar school, as a preparatory step to a learned profession. What did he there? He studied some, but used his pencil more. Drawing was to him a fascinating amusement, and a study which he could pursue with more intensity than he could bring to bear upon the dead languages. No doubt, his classical knowledge was afterwards eminently useful.

But he must and would be an artist, in spite of the opposition and harshness of his father and other relations, who feared Michel would thus degrade the dignity of the family. That circumstance alone rescued the family name from oblivion, and gave it a lasting place in the temple of fame.

The father of the immortal Raffaelle,† another architect and painter, was a painter. He bestowed great care upon the

*Michel Angelo Buonorotti, born in Tuscany, A. D. 1474.

†Raffaelle Sanzio, born at Urbino in the Papal States, A. D. 1483.

early education of his only son. One of Raffaelle's biographers says: "with the maternal milk Raffaelle seems to have imbibed the taste for painting. His first playthings were the implements of his father's art. From the time the child could walk he was made the companion and the assistant of his father's labors."

"No man is born into the world, whose work is not born with him; there is always work, and *tools* to work withal, for those who will." So thought Benjamin West,* when he seized *pen and ink*, and sketched a likeness of his baby-sister as she smiled in her cradle. So thought he, when he purloined the hair from the cat's back, and drew it through a goose-quill to make a paint-brush. The colors Benjamin used were charcoal and chalk, mixed with the juice of berries; truly, this *ingenuity* in a boy of six or seven years of age, who had never seen either picture, brush, or pencil, was a sufficient indication that he was born to be a painter. "Tools to work withal!" Who else would have found them? Even the Mohawk Indians, the neighbors of Benjamin West, had better materials. A party of them visited Springfield; they saw the boy's paintings, and supplied him with red and yellow ochre, to which his mother added the gift of a piece of *indigo*. And now Benjamin became a portrait-painter; his likenesses sold for a dollar apiece, and excited the wonder and admiration of the inhabitants of Western Pennsylvania.

* Benjamin West, born at Springfield, Penn., A. D. 1738.

The painter Fuseli* when about ten years old "bought with his small allowance of pocket money, candles, pencils and paper, in order to make drawings at night." These he sold to his companions, and the produce enabled him either to purchase materials for the execution of other drawings, or to add articles to his own wardrobe. The subjects he chose for his pictures were either terrific or ludicrous scenes, in both these, he at all periods of life excelled. While his father was reading the son was not unfrequently employed in drawing with his left hand, and this practice gave him a free use of that hand during his life. The father of Fuseli resolutely determined that his son should not be an artist; he would not even allow him to draw for amusement. He was to be made a clergyman, *nolens volens;* a clergyman in spite of his entire unfitness for that sacred office, and his decided talents for a painter.

Thus, the benefits of an early artistic education were denied to Fuseli, and when in after years he became a painter by profession, the deficiencies resulting from this want of culture were evident in all his works. His biographer says: "From this circumstance his early works have figures short in stature, with muscular but clumsy limbs. His talents were checked by the freaks of an ungovernable fancy, which seldom suffered him to finish his work. Though Fuseli invented and composed with great rapidity, he never learned the proper use of colors. He daubed them on in a dry pow-

*Henry Fuseli was born at Zurich, in Switzerland, A. D. 1741.

dered state mixed up with a quantity of oil, spirits of turpentine and gold size, and depended for the effect of his pictures upon their spirited design, rather than their mechanical execution." These facts are mentioned here, to show the importance to an artist of a right beginning. Goethe says, "color-grinding has been the first step of many eminent artists, and that it is of immense importance that the artist should take hold of Art by the right side. The *practice* of the imitative arts is mechanical, and the cultivation of the Artist begins naturally, in his earliest years, with the mechanical."

Canova,* the most celebrated sculptor of modern times, lost his father when he was only three years old. Soon after, his mother married again, and the boy went to live with his grandparents. Canova's grandfather was a stonecutter, and the little boy amused himself with making models in clay of various objects, and chiselling bits of marble and stone, with his tiny hand, into forms which were proofs of genius. His imagination was excited by the ballads and tales which his grandmother related, and to which it was his delight to listen.

At the age of eight, Canova was employed as a workman in his grandfather's shop, and continued in his employment until twelve years of age. The story has been told, of Canova's having attracted the notice of a distinguished nobleman, by making a butter-lion for one of his entertain-

* Canova was born in the Venitian Territory, A. D. 1757.

ments. How Canova came to be on the lucky spot, just when an ornament was wanted for the nobleman's table, does not appear; but the story goes, that the boy seized the opportunity to distinguish himself, and made such a spirited animal in butter, that it recommended him to the notice of the Signor Falieri, who afterwards became his patron. This story may be true, and it may not; it has been generally received as a fact.

Thomas Bewick,* a celebrated wood-engraver, when very young was accustomed to delineate animals with surprising accuracy and spirit. He had no instruction, and what is termed an accident, led to the discovery of his uncommon talents. With a piece of chalk, he amused himself by drawing bold sketches on the doors and walls of houses in the little village of Cherryburn, where he lived. A copper-plate-engraver, who was passing through the village, was so much surprised and pleased at the genius displayed by the young artist, that he sought him out and proposed to his father to take the boy for an apprentice; the proposal was gladly accepted.

The late lamented Washington Allston† has given some exceedingly interesting reminiscences of his childhood. "To go back as far as I can," said he, "I remember that I used to draw before I left Carolina at six years of age, and still

* Born in Northumberland, England, in 1753; died in 1828.

† Washington Allston was born in the State of South Carolina, A. D. 1779, and died in Cambridge, Mass., A. D. 1844.

earlier, that my favorite amusement, much akin to it, was making little landscapes about the roots of an old tree in the country—meagre enough, no doubt; the only particulars of which I can call to mind, were a cottage built of sticks, shaded by little trees, which were composed of the small suckers (I think so called,) resembling miniature trees, which I gathered in the woods. Another employment was the converting the stalks of the wild ferns into little men and women, by winding about them different colored yarn. These were sometimes presented with pitchers made of the pomegranate flower. *These childish fancies were the straws by which, perhaps, an observer might then have guessed which way the current was setting for after life.*"

Dunlap remarks, that in these delights of Allston's childhood appear the germs of landscape gardening, landscape painting, sculpture and scenic composition. Less intellectual children are content to make mud pies, and form ovens of clay and clam-shells as if to bake them in; even when at play, they are haunted by the ghosts of cakes, pies and puddings. Allston was a poet as well as a painter, and he has recorded the fact that his imagination was active and vivid in early childhood. The delight which he took in sketching and making miniature gardens, men and women, he says "would sometimes give way to a stronger love for the wild and the marvellous. I delighted in being terrified by the tales of witches and hags, which the negroes used to tell me; and I well remember with how much pleasure I recalled these feelings on my return to Carolina, especially on revisiting a gigantic wild grape-vine in the wood, which had been the favorite swing for one of these witches."

Like all persons of delicate sensibility, and a tincture of romance, Allston looked back with intense interest to the days of childhood. He remarks, that in after life, when the hey-day of youth is past, "the gentler emotions are to the man as early friends who revisit him in dreams. And how beautiful is this law of nature, perfuming, as it were, our very graves with the unheeded flowers of childhood. One of my favorite haunts, when a child in Carolina, was a forest-spring where I used to catch minnows, and I dare say with all the callousness of a fisherman; at this moment I can see that spring, and the pleasant conjuror, memory, has brought again those little creatures before me; but how unlike to what they were! They seem to me like the spirits of the woods, which a flash from their little diamond eyes lights up afresh, in all their gorgeous garniture of leaves and flowers."

James Barry* was of humble parentage. His father was the master of a small vessel in which he carried on a petty trade between England and Ireland. When very young James was taken on board this vessel as cabin-boy, a disgusting occupation to him who had received a tolerably good education. Whenever he could find time he employed himself in sketching upon the deck natural objects. He

*Born at Cork, in Ireland, 1741.

possessed no better means for this than chalk or ochre. Yet the eye of one accustomed to works of art would have discovered upon the rough deck the talents of the childish draftsman. His father finding that James was so passionately fond of painting that it would be useless to attempt making him a sailor, allowed him to return home and go again to school.

One of the earliest American sculptors, Horatio Greenough,* in "the manufacture of his playthings early manifested a love of the beauty of form." Many of his amusements were of a nature to show a decided propensity for the profession which he finally chose.

His schoolfellows often begged of him to carve them wood cimiters and daggers, as every one he made surpassed the last in beauty.

His brother says, "I recollect in particular, a small pocket-pistol of his manufacture, which was cast of lead, and mounted on a very gracefully formed stock inlaid with flowers and ornamental work of thin strips of lead, which had when new the appearance of silver."

"I might mention numerous instances of this kind, but will merely speak of one more favorite amusement. This was the manufacture of little carriages and horses, with drivers of beeswax of different colors, which being very small, (the wheels of the circumference of a cent,) were the admiration of all our visitors, for their beauty and delicacy. The carriages

* Born in Boston, 1805; died Dec. 18, 1852.

were formed on exceedingly graceful models, trimmed and lined with bits of silk and gold cord, and with the horses which were well modelled, had quite the air of the equipages of some Lilliputian noble.

"A small room was, by the consent of our parents, appropriated for the manufacture and preservation of these articles, and invention soon suggested the idea of laying out, on long pine tables, estates for the supposed proprietors of these equipages. The houses and stables were laid out, as it were, on a ground plan merely, the apartments being divided like pews in a church, by partitions made of drawing paper, and furnished with miniature articles of similar manufacture; and in this room, and with these puppets, adventures were dramatically gone through, with great enthusiasm, in play hours, for nearly *two years*, when the system having arrived at what seemed the *ne plus ultra*, was abandoned for some new project."

The celebrated Cole, *the* American Landscape painter, was "fond of drawing from his infancy, and passionately devoted to the contemplation of the scenery of nature. An excessive bashfulness, joined to this love of the combination of land, water and sky, which the ordinary eye may be said not to see, caused him to avoid the society not only of adults, but of children of his own age—he sought and found in nature the pleasure which seemed denied him elsewhere. To ramble through the woods, or on the beautiful banks of the Ohio, indulging in day-dreams, was the apparently idle occupation of a most active mind of one who has proved a most persevering and industrious practitioner and student of nature's lessons."

Thorwaldsen* the sculptor was the son of a poor wood-carver, who made figure-heads for vessels. Few ships came to the inhospitable shores of Iceland, and the father was scarcely able to keep his wife and children from perishing with cold and hunger. After a fierce struggle with poverty, he decided to remove to Copenhagen where he would find employment enough for the support of himself and family.

After their arrival in Copenhagen another son was born, Albert, who has since become so celebrated as a sculptor. The father was obliged still to work very hard at his trade. While thus employed he was frequently amused to see his fair-haired, beautiful boy, watching him with intense interest.

As soon as Albert could handle a chisel, he began to carve little images of various kinds from the refuse wood in his father's shop. The poor man was not able to send his son to school, and day after day the child sat in a corner of the shop busy with his childish play. And yet this childish play was truly the beginning of his apprenticeship to the beautiful art of sculpture. The blue eyes of the fair boy dilated with pleasure when his father at length noticed and praised his carving. He not only praised the boy but allowed him to assist in carving figure-heads.

It happened, when Albert was eleven years old, that his

* Born about 1775, in Copenhagen.

father was seized with an illness which prevented him from executing a figure-head which he had engaged to an old ship-captain. Albert Thorwaldsen determined without the knowledge of his father to do the work himself. It was to represent the head of a woman. The child worked zealously at the rough wooden block till the head was completed. When the father returned to his shop, lo, there, as if done by magic, was the figure-head! Albert was alarmed lest his father should blame his rashness, and blushing and trembling confessed the secret. The carver was delighted, and assured the child that he could not have done it half so well himself.

The old sailor was in raptures, and declared that the boy would one day be a great man, and he should be very proud of having Albert Thorwaldsen's work on the ship Ulrika.

One more instance of the early development of genius remains to be mentioned, though thousands might be adduced to prove that there is a special aptitude for the fine arts, the indications of which cannot be mistaken.

Sir Thomas Lawrence,* without having his taste or inclination directed in any way whatever towards painting, and consequently without the slightest instruction, at the age of four or five years began to paint likenesses. Even at that early age it was remarked that he excelled in the drawing of the eye; and this was characteristic of him when he became the most celebrated portrait painter of modern times.

At the age of seven the youthful Lawrence had excited

* Born at Bristol, England, 1769; died, 1830.

general attention, and his portraits were universally admired. At ten he was so celebrated as to be noticed with strong panegyric by the Hon. D. Barrington in his "Miscellanies."

It was about this time that the father of Lawrence removed to Weymouth, where the youthful son continued to practice portrait-painting and occasionally attempted original Historical pictures. Another change brought him to Bath; at the age of thirteen, he was the most popular portrait painter in that city, and from this time his father and all his family depended upon him for support.

## CHAPTER III.

### THE CHILDHOOD OF THE ARTIST.

"Men, my brothers, men the workers, ever reaping something new;
That which they have done, but *earnest of the things that they shall do.*"

TENNYSON.

ONE of the best English landscape painters, Gainsborough,* while a young school-boy, used to steal away to a beautiful wood, and sketch in his copy-book, flowers, trees, and other natural objects. It is said that these infantile sketches were strikingly like the mature performances of after years. At the age of ten he was skillful in sketching, and at twelve he was so decidedly a painter that no doubts were entertained about his future destination.

"On one occasion, Gainsborough was concealed among some bushes in his father's garden, making a sketch of an old fantastic tree, when he observed a man looking most wistfully over the wall at some pears, which were hanging ripe and tempting. The slanting light of the sun happened to throw the eager face into a highly picturesque mixture of light and shade, and Tom immediately sketched his likeness, much to the poor man's consternation afterwards, and much to the amusement of Tom's father when he taxed the

* Thomas Gainsborough was born in Suffolk, in 1727.

peasant with the intention of plundering his garden, and showed him how he then looked. No fine clump of trees, no picturesque stream, nor romantic glade—no cattle grazing, nor flocks reposing, nor peasants pursuing their rural or pastoral occupations, escaped his diligent pencil. *Those hasty sketches were all treasured up as materials to be used when his hand should have become more skillful.* His *first* drawing was a clump of trees, and one of his biographers says it was 'a wonderful thing.'"

This early development of artistic talent was not to be mistaken. Tom's father was persuaded to send him to London, for the benefit of instruction, and he left Ludbury for the metropolis at the age of fourteen.

The English sculptor, Flaxman,* was a weakly child, and slightly deformed from his birth, and yet he is described as possessing "a serene temper and an enthusiastic mind."

His father kept a small shop in New street, Covent Garden, London, for the sale of plaster figures.

John was too feeble to join in the boisterous plays of healthful children, and was left to devise amusement for his solitary hours.

The patient little boy would sit hour after hour in a little stuffed chair by his father's counter, and draw from the plaster models with black chalk. This amusement he mingled with reading, for which he had an early and intense fondness.

* John Flaxman, born in York, England, A. D. 1755.

The customers who frequented his father's shop noticed with surprise the grave and cheerful manner of this sickly child, and were pleased with his drawings. They questioned him about his reading, and listened with astonishment to his ready and appropriate answers. When they spoke of poets and sculptors, his eye kindled and his pale face flushed with emotion. Not contented with copying the figures around him, he had read parts of Homer and had attempted to design from the poet's description. One of his biographers tells the following anecdote:

Flaxman's father was going to see the procession at the coronation of George III, and the child begged earnestly that he would bring him one of the medals which were to be thrown to the populace. He was not fortunate enough to get one, but on his way home, happening to find a plated button bearing the stamp of a horse and jockey, rather than wholly disappoint his little boy, who was then in a very delicate state of health, he ventured to deceive him, and gave him the button. John took it and was thankful, but remarked, "It is a very odd device for a coronation medal." He was then five years old. At this age he was fond of examining the seals of every watch he saw, and kept a bit of soft wax to take an impression of any which pleased him. When some one reminded Flaxman of this after he had become eminent, he replied, "Sir, *we are never too young to learn what is useful, nor too old to grow wise and good.*" The Rev. Mr. Mathew relates another characteristic anecdote: "I went," said the clergyman, "to the shop of old Flaxman to have a figure repaired, and while I was standing there, I heard a child cough behind the counter, I looked over, and there I saw a little boy seated on a small chair, with a large chair before him, on which lay a book he was reading. His fine eyes and beautiful forehead interested me, and I said, 'What book is that?' He raised himself on his crutches, bowed and said, 'Sir, it is a Latin book, and I am trying to learn it.' 'Aye, indeed,' I exclaimed, 'you are a fine boy; but this is not the proper book. I'll bring you the right one to-morrow.' I did as I promised, and the acquaintance, thus casually begun, ripened into one of the best friendships of my life."

Who can say that the childhood of the feeble solitary boy was, after all, less happy than that of other apparently favored children. The wise law of compensation, equalizes the condition of mankind in a wonderful manner. The infant sculptor found pleasure in modelling in plaster of Paris, wax, and clay, while his companions in age were building mud forts in the alley, or making sand pies in the court-yard.

Health, however, the indispensable blessing of humanity, had hitherto been denied him. He could not move without crutches, and long fits of illness interrupted his studies and his favorite pursuits. He had seldom seen the green fields and shady groves of the country, and the blank walls of the city shut out even the glorious canopy of heaven. But when John was nine years of age, a delightful change took place in his condition. Health flushed his thoughtful face with her roseate hues; his limbs became strong and active. The crutches were gladly thrown aside, never again to be needed by the happy boy.

His enthusiasm and love of romance were strongly developed. His mind was filled with the adventures of the heroes of chivalry, and he longed to become a knight-errant. This romantic fervor was increased, rather than diminished, by reading Don Quixote.

"He was so much delighted with the amiable though eccentric hero, and his account of the duties and perils of knight-errantry, that he thought he could not do better than sally forth to right wrongs and redress grievances. Accordingly, one morning early, unknown to any one, armed with a little French sword, he set out, without a squire, in search of adventures—which he could not find. After wandering about Hyde Park the whole day without meeting enchanter or distressed damsel, he returned home rather ashamed of his romantic flight, and never again sought to emulate the exploits of him of La Mancha, though he always retained a great admiration of his character."

And now that health and strength were confirmed, the youthful Flaxman resolved to be a Sculptor. From the models in his father's shop, he modelled and drew most industriously, and thus gained a knowledge of form and proportion.

In a moment of confidence the youthful artist showed one Mortimer, a painter, a drawing of a human eye:

"Is it an oyster?" inquired Mortimer. This joke made a deep impression upon the sensitive, enthusiastic child, and wisely did he resolve to show no more of his attempts "to those who consider it wisdom to humble the enthusiasm of youthful genius."

His consciousness of power was not to be shaken by a sneer; his determination to be an Artist was not to be changed by a few spiteful words. "He had resolved to do something by which his name might be continued to the world."

Some time after John Flaxman had attracted the notice of the Rev. Mr. Mathew, he became a frequent visitor at the house of that gentleman, whose wife was the friend of Mrs. Montague, Mrs. Chapone, and Mrs. Barbauld.

"He was eleven years old when he first saw Mrs. Mathew, and to her house he thenceforth frequently repaired during the evenings, to hear her read Homer and Virgil, and discourse upon sculpture and verse. Here he was encouraged in studying the dead languages, so necessary to him in his profession. His mode of education was very desultory; he attended no college; he distinguished himself in no eminent seminary; he gathered his knowledge from many sources, and mastered what he wanted by some of those ready methods which form part of the inspiration of genius.

"Mrs. Mathew read Homer to him, and commented upon

the pictorial beauty of his poetry, while Flaxman sat beside her, sketching such passages as caught his fancy. Those juvenile productions still exist, and are touched, and that not slightly, with the quiet loveliness and serene vigor manifested long afterwards in his famous illustrations of the same poet.

"The praise bestowed on those early and imperfect works, was grateful to the young artist; friends, more merciful, or more wise in their criticisms, than Mortimer, now foretold his future eminence. But excellence in art, they warned him, was not to be attained without serious study, and assiduously working in the spirit of his own nature—by musing on the heroic and lofty, and seeking to stamp on his conceptions, that universal beauty acknowledged by all nations."

In his fifteenth year, Flaxman became a student of the Royal Academy, and the same year exhibited there a figure of Neptune in wax. Fifty seven years after, he exhibited at the same place, a statue of John Kemble. All this period was devoted with intense earnestness to that pursuit, which had been the deliberate choice of his infant mind.

One of the most remarkable instances of early development was that of George Morland.* His father was a very indifferent painter, and to better his pecuniary affairs, entered into speculation. Entirely failing in this attempt, he became quite indigent. The son, George, as early as the

* Born in London, 1763.

age of four years, began to use the pencil and crayon with dexterity; and at the age of five and six, his drawings were purchased with avidity by persons to whom they were exhibited. The money thus received induced the needy father to take a very unwise and wicked course. He confined George to a garret, shut out from the blessed air of heaven, and taxed both body and mind, most unmercifully. By the time that he was fourteen, he had formed those habits which threw a dark shadow over his after life. There, in that lonely garret, the boy made the drawings which his father greedily seized upon and sold. There, too, was laid the foundation for the vice and misery of his future life. The father pampered his appetite for food and drink, and indulged him to excess. Think of a boy, ten years of age, laboring from day to day for the support of his family! The sports of childhood were denied him, and often must he have sighed and dropped bitter tears upon his drawings, as the joyous shouts of boys let loose from school, reached his solitary apartment.

After a while, he learned to steal away from that garret and mingle with low companions, in dark alleys and dirty courts. To obtain money, he secreted some of his own drawings and gave the remainder to his father. The money he obtained for his clever pictures, was spent in coarse amusement, carousing, singing and joking at the tavern.

## CHAPTER IV.

### THE YOUTH OF THE ARTIST.

"Genius without bias, is a stream without direction; it inundates all, and ends in stagnation."—*Fuseli.*

THE childhood of the Artist is past. How is he so to employ boyhood and youth that manhood may fulfil the promise of chilhood?

"Art is long and time is fleeting;"

And the sand as it glides through the hour-glass may be bright and golden, or dull and sombre as that of the lazy hermit in his cheerless cell.

The "airy shapes" which Imagination bodies forth, must have a "local habitation" upon the canvas—must become permanent in marble, or have a firm foundation upon the solid earth, and demonstrate to coming ages the genius and skill of the immortal artist. In order to accomplish such works, *skill* must be acquired by long and patient practice. The *hand* must be taught to obey the will and to execute what the mind conceives.

Albert Durer* had wonderful facility of hand. A brother artist once asked him for the pencil with which he drew hair

* Albert Durer was born in Germany, A. D. 1471.

so minutely; "Durer held out to him a handful of every kind, telling him to take any one he liked as he could do it with them all." Once, in a party of artists, when every one was giving a proof of his skill, Durer took a piece of chalk and drew quite off-hand a circle on the table, telling them that they might bring compasses and measure it; which being done, it was found to the astonishment of all present that he had hit it to a hair.

This reminds one of the contest between the ancient Grecian painters, Protogenes and Apelles, as related by Pliny. Protogenes resided at Rhodes where Apelles went to pay him a visit. The former was absent from home, but Apelles requested to be shown into the atelier of the artist. Upon a piěce of canvas already stretched for a picture, Apelles drew a *line* and left it, as his only card. He needed no other, for Protogenes when he saw it, declared that no one but Apelles could have drawn that line. With the emulation natural to a man of genius, Portogenes drew a line more perfect, and directed that when the stranger called again he should be again admitted to the atelier. Apelles came, and with surprise saw that his line had been excelled. He instantly drew a third line, which, Protogenes, when he saw it, declared could not be excelled. The canvas upon which these famous lines were drawn was carefully preserved, and so highly valued that it was long after carried to Rome and placed in the palace of the Cæsars. It is impossible now, even to conjecture in what the excellence of those lines consisted. They doubtless exhibited that astonishing facility of hand and accuracy of sight, which alone can give grace, precision and proportion, essential requisites to the production of beauty. No line of the human figure can be produced by any known law, like that by which a circle or a square can be drawn; the same is true of the scroll of the Ionic capital; hence, the perfect skill which the hand must possess to dash off the outline of what the eye sees, or the mind conceives. The Artist is to bring to the aid of achievement the same industry and perseverance indispensable in other pursuits. He is not to work like the poor beast in a treadmill, or the man whose bones muscles and sinews are only a piece of complicated mechanism for other minds to use and direct.*

The Artist, it is true, labors with the hand, but what guides that hand to the execution of noble works? Genius, talent, taste. Minerva sprang from the head of Jupiter armed *cap-a-pie*. Not so with genius. She inherits godlike power but

* Dr. Tucker, the famous Dean of Gloucester, asserted before the Society for Encouraging Commerce and Manufactures, that a pin-maker was a more useful and valuable member of society than Raphael, the painter. Sir Joshua Reynolds was nettled at this remark, and replied with some asperity: "This is an observation of a very narrow mind, a mind that is confined to the mere object of commerce—that sees with a microscopic eye but a part of the great machine of the economy of life, and thinks that small part which he sees to be the whole. Commerce is the means, not the end, of happiness and pleasure; the end is a rational enjoyment by means of arts and sciences. It is, therefore, the highest degree of folly to set the means in a higher rank of esteem than the end. It is as much as to say, that the brick-maker is superior to the architect."

comes by slow degrees and much toil, to the full possession of her inheritance. The millions of movements of which the hand is capable render it the most wonderful and most powerful of all instruments. It will not, however, obey the will without training. The youth of the artist is the time for acquiring this perfect command of the instrument he is to employ. The eye, too, must be educated. There may be an original, keen perception of natural harmonies in coloring, but philosophical enquiry and constant observation will quicken and improve this perception. "The education we miss in youth we rarely attain in age." This adage is eminently true with regard to the education of the hand and eye. The same faults in drawing, or the same bad coloring which glared out from the earliest productions of the painter, too frequently, are visible amid the richness and beauty of his maturer works.

*Patient, well directed labor* in youth, will alone give that power over the hand, and that accuracy and correctness of eye, without which genius is like Mercury robbed of his winged cap and *talaria.**

* It will probably be remembered, that the *petasus*, and the *talaria*, enabled the god, Mercury, to go with inconceivable swiftness to every part of the universe, and to assume whatever shape he pleased.

# CHAPTER V.

## WARNINGS.

"To the young and inexperienced, lessons of warning are as necessary as lessons of encouragement."

Genius is oftentimes sensitive and shy; it exaggerates difficulties from without; it places itself in opposition to the whole world; it conjures up giants and dragons, before whom it crouches in dismay. Then, again, it is bold and reckless; it assumes superiority over other minds; it claims no kindred with common sense. It defies mankind.

Disastrous has been the delusion, that genius would make its irresistible way without the aid of good sense and moral worth. Dark and mournful the catalogue of gifted men whose vices and follies made them, while on earth, even more conspicuous than their genius, and now serve as a fearful warning. Far more noble might have been the works of art which "live after them," had they kept the pure light of genius unsullied by folly and sin.

The Artist lives in a world of his own. There, he reigns a despot. When he comes into collision with the world of reality, he does not like its men and women. They are totally unlike the creations of his own fancy. They do not like him. They do not acknowledge his right to stand apart from them and claim endowments in which they cannot share. He contends for these rights, and frequently in a manner so violent and disagreeable, as to offend and disgust.

The painter Fuseli, when in college, "discovered and exposed weak points in some of the professors and tutors who had been held up as examples to the students. If he could not obtain his object by satire, in which he was very powerful, he sometimes resorted to caricature, a weapon not less formidable in his hands. The wounded pride of some of the masters induced them to draw up a formal complaint against him, and he was threatened with expulsion by the president."

He afterwards got himself into difficulty with the magistrates of Zurich, and was obliged to quit his native land.

He seemed to take special pleasure in exposing the faults and foibles of persons with whom he associated. He was accustomed to meet Dr. Geddes, at the house of Mr. Johnson, the publisher, in London. Both Fuseli and the Doctor, "from their natural temperament, were impatient of contradiction, and each had an opinion of his own powers, and depreciated those of the other. It was only to meet, in order to dispute, and the ready wit of Fuseli raised the irritable temper of the Doctor, who, when provoked, would burst out of the room and walk once or twice round Saint Paul's Churchyard, before he returned to the company, to the great amusement of Fuseli." Of course the Doctor became his enemy.

"When Fuseli tendered himself for the office of Keeper of the Royal Academy, Northcote and Opie voted against him; but they considered it right to call upon him the day after his election, to explain their motives. After having heard them, and in their explanation they in some degree blamed each other, he answered, in his usual sarcastic manner: 'I am sorry you have taken this trouble, because I shall lose my character in the neighborhood. When you entered my house, the one must have been taken for a little Jew creditor, the other for a bum-bailiff; so, good morning.'"

Could there have been a more ungracious reception of two brother artists, who came to make the *amende honorable!*

His irritability in one instance, nearly cost him his life. At Lyons, when a young man, he had a dispute with a person, which aroused his feelings to such a height, that in a momentary fit of passion, he made use of that agility which he possessed, and kicked his antagonist in the face. The man coolly drew his sword, and immediately inflicted a very severe wound upon the offending leg. He possessed such a degree of pride and self-love, that if he thought himself slighted, he would resent it, whatever might be the rank or condition of the man.

Such a man as Fuseli, is a dangerous enemy and a very unsafe friend. The painter, Barry,* affords another example in point. "His masculine energy and hardihood of

* James Barry, born at Cork, in 1741.

nature, from having been allowed to grow up undisciplined, very early degenerated into a species of recklessness and ferocity, which proved the blight of his genius, and the curse of his existence. His arrogance and infirmity of temper, as well as his imprudence and his extraordinary ignorance of the world, showed themselves almost in the very commencement of his career. Scarcely had Barry set his foot in Rome, whither he went to improve himself in art, than he discovered (to his own satisfaction) that all the principles and maxims there recognized with regard to the art he came to study, were stupidly wrong, and he forthwith not only denounced them as such, but quarreled with everybody who chose to stand up in their defence. From the same spirit of opposition and contumacy, he would not, while there, pursue the same method of study as his brother artists, but, instead of employing himself in making drawings of the works of the great masters with his hand, he satisfied himself with taking fac-similies of them with an instrument. He even spent much of his time in the investigation of subjects hardly connected, at all, with his proper occupation. All this time he had, in his friend Burke,* an invaluable monitor, whose counsels continued to be tendered till the last, with a frankness, and, at the same time, a delicacy in the manner, only equalled by the admirable wisdom of the matter.

* Edmund Burke, one of the most profound statesmen Great Britain has ever produced.

But although Barry felt the kindness, and, at times, even the good sense of the advice he received, it certainly produced no effect upon his conduct. On his return to England, he acted in the same manner as he had done at Rome, attacking and quarreling with every body, insisting upon having his own way in every thing, too often apparently out of a spirit of selfishness, or the mere love of dispute and opposition; and, in short, in his whole conduct, regarding nothing save his own humors and impetuous impulses. To deport himself after this fashion, he seems to have thought, was a privilege he possessed as a man of genius—a weak mistake, *which, if his genius had been of the highest kind, he never would have fallen into*. How much truer course, than that which his own ill-regulated temper and childish notions of dignity suggested to him, might he have found in a few sentences of one of the letters addressed to him by Burke, a short time before he returned from Italy:

"Believe me, my dear Barry," writes this considerate friend, "that the arms, with which the ill dispositions of the world are to be combated, and the qualities by which it is to be reconciled to us, and we reconciled to it, are moderation, gentleness, a little indulgence to others, and a great deal of distrust of ourselves; which are not qualities of a mean spirit, as some may possibly think them, but virtues of a great and noble kind, and such as dignify our nature as much as they contribute to our repose and fortune; for nothing can be so unworthy of a well-composed soul, as to pass away life in bickerings and litigations; in snarling and scuffling with every one about us. Again and again, my dear Barry, we must be at peace with our species, if not for their sakes, yet very much for our own."

"Leonardo Da Vinci,"* says the painter Fuseli, "broke forth with a splendor which distanced former excellence. Made up of all the elements that constitute the essence of genius, favored by education and circumstances, all ear, all eye, all grasp; painter, poet, sculptor, anatomist, architect, engineer, chemist, machinist, musician, man of science, and sometimes empiric, he laid hold of every beauty in the enchanted circle, but without exclusive attachment to one, dismissed, in her turn, each. *Fitter to scatter hints than teach by example, he wasted life, insatiate, in experiment.* To a capacity which at once penetrated the principle and real aim of art, he joined an inequality of fancy that at one moment lent him wings for the pursuit of beauty, and the next, flung him on the ground to crawl after deformity. His notions of the most elaborate finish, and *his want of perseverance,* were at least equal. His Last Supper in the Refectory of the Dominicans at Milano, was the only one of Leonardo's great works which he carried to ultimate finish through all its parts."

The youth of George Morland was such as might have been expected from the striking indications of his childhood. At the age of sixteen, he contrived to break loose from

*Leonardo da Vinci, is said to have died at Paris, in 1517, aged 75.

his father, and to march off, dressed in his favorite green coat and top-boots, carrying with him his pallet, easel, and pencils. "He was in the very extreme of puppyism; his head, when ornamented according to his own taste, re-resembled a snowball, to which was attached a short thick *queue,* not unlike a painter's brush. Thus accoutered, with little money in his pocket, and a large conceit of himself, George Morland made an excursion to Margate, with the two-fold purpose of enjoying *life* and painting portraits.

His skill of hand was great; his facility, it is said, wondrous; while his oddity of dress, his extreme youth, and the story of his early studies, attracted curiosity and attention. Sitters came—the wealthy and the beautiful. But *the painter loved low company;* all that was polished or genteel, was the object of his dislike.

Horse-jockeys, money-lenders, hostlers and pugilists, were his boon companions, and with them he roamed about by land and water. It is astonishing that his genius did not go out in utter darkness. His subjects were such as might have been expected from the circumstances, but they were dashed off with spirit, and true to life; so true was his pencil, that he drew landscapes with a "close dogged fidelity, which claims the merit of looking like some known spot, where pigs prowl, cattle graze, or asses browse." Pigs and asses were indeed the favorites which he preferred to titled ladies, and well-dressed gentlemen. Morland fell in love and married "a young lady of beauty and modesty."

She believed he had reformed, for he did awhile suspend his habits of dissipation. But very soon after marriage, in spite of the remonstrances of his wife, his darling sins broke loose and made him again a captive to their relentless tyranny.

Poverty and the jail followed. He painted still with facility, solely for the purpose of obtaining money, which he squandered with the most lavish profusion.

He had at last become so well known for his genius and his dissipation, that any story of distress about him, would be credited, so that "anecdotes of Morland, the painter," are said to have been regularly manufactured for newspapers and magazines.

"This ill-fated artist seemed to have possessed two minds; one, the animated soul of genius, by which he rose in his profession ; and the other, that debased and grovelling propensity which condemned him to the very abyss of dissipation. Such a man could not "live out half his days." His constitution was ruined, and his personal character was held in general contempt. No one would associate with him but the meanest of mankind. His gradual descent in society may be traced in the productions of his pencil; yet, his wonderful skill of hand and sense of the picturesque did not forsake him, until that hand was paralyzed by disease, and that prolific brain darkened by the shadows of death. He died in utter wretchedness and penury, the saddest example on record, of the abuse of genius."

## CHAPTER VI.

### ENCOURAGEMENT.

"Know what thou hast to do, and do it."—*Turner.*

"Even the hound runs himself to death after the hare, if his master only says to him, 'thou art a brave *Apollo.*' So it is also with the Artist. These words—'thou hast painted a good picture'—satisfies his heart, for he has honestly done that which the Lord has given him ability to do."—*Artist's Married Life.*

THE sculptor, Canova, whose early developed talent introduced him to the notice of the noble Falieri family, has been already mentioned. Whether the incident related of the butter-lion be true or not, it is certain, that while Canova was industriously working in the stone-cutter's shop of his grandfather, he became known to that family. It was ascertained, beyond the possibility of doubt, that the boy had uncommon genius for sculpture, and Count Falieri sent him to an artist named Toretto, to receive instruction in the art of sculpture. It is probable that his patron expected no more than that Canova would be thus enabled to follow the trade of his father and grandfather, who were stone-cutters. If so, the boy took him by surprise, by acquiring far more than was intended.

After Canova had worked diligently in the shop of his master Toretto, for more than a year, he was one day seized with a desire to accomplish what might long have been floating in his busy brain. The master being absent, Canova modeled two angels in clay. What was the surprise of Toretto on beholding these figures! He had only taught the youthful artist the mechanical part of sculpture; under the pupil's plastic hand two angels had been formed from clay. The master might have shaken his head in despair, had it been required of him to execute a similar work. Yet Canova remained with Toretto about three years, and then went back to follow the trade of a stone-cutter in his native village.

Signor Falieri, meantime, had removed to Venice, and it is possible that some beautiful work of art, in that splendid city, may have reminded him of the early promise of his protege. He sent for the boy to come to him, and Canova obeyed. The artist was now in his sixteenth year. Earnestly did he avail himself of the glorious opportunities now offered him. In the academies and galleries of Venice he passed his mornings studying the works of art; the evenings he devoted to the general improvement of his mind; but, in the afternoon, he was daily found plying the mallet and chisel in the workshop of a sculptor. He resided in the palace of Signor Falieri, but he did not wish to be entirely dependent upon his patron.

"I labored for a mere pittance," said Canova, in a letter to a friend written years afterwards; "I labored for a mere pittance, but it was sufficient. It was the fruit of my own resolution; and as I then thought, the foretaste of more honorable rewards, for I never thought of wealth."

His earliest performances in sculpture may still be seen in Venice.

Canova after a while set up his own shop. It was a small cell under the monastery of the Augustine Friars. For four years Canova labored indefatigably in that obscure place. There, though little noticed, he was rapidly advancing in his chosen art.

There "he first began to perceive the necessity of founding the study of art upon the study of nature, in opposition to the notion which then prevailed, that certain assumed principles and rules of operation were alone to be attended to." As soon as this new view dawned upon his mind he hastened to regulate his studies in conformity to it.

Instead of merely examining and copying the works of other sculptors, he resorted, for every part of his art, to the works of nature.

He studied anatomy. He attended the public spectacles and the theatres, that he might catch the finest attitudes of the human figure from the living exhibition.

In walking the streets, in like manner, his eye was constantly on the watch, to catch new forms of grace and power from the life around him. His art now became, more than ever, the sole object for which he lived. He laid down a rule for himself, which he strictly observed, *never to pass a day without making some progress*, or retire to rest till he had produced some design.

In the mean time he also pursued with ardor his studies

in general knowledge, especially in those branches which he conceived to be most important to him in his profession; such as poetry, antiquities, and the Greek and Roman classics, which, however, he could only read through the medium of translations. He also studied the French and Spanish languages.

There, in that humble cell, did the great sculptor go through with the true apprenticeship for life. Very little known to the busy world, was he, who was thus preparing to become one of the most celebrated men of modern times. In 1776, (at the age of nineteen,) he exhibited his finished group of Orpheus and Eurydice, and from that time orders for statuary flowed in from various quarters.

He soon after removed from his cell to a more appropriate studio. Thus had he accomplished childhood and youth; his manhood will bear ample testimony to the excellence of fruit produced from such blossoming and ripening.

When Benjamin West was a small school-boy he drew a ship on the smooth sand which delighted and astonished his school-fellows. One of them exclaimed "time and chance happen to all, and you will be a great man yet."

This prediction made a deep impression upon the mind of West. He resolved that it should be accomplished, yet well he knew that not chance, but application, must make him the predicted great man. The goose quill, with its brush of cat's hair, the charcoal, chalk, juice of berries, and indigo, which the child had used, were thrown aside by the boy; for a kind friend sent him a box of paints and brushes, and canvas stretched upon frames, ready for the youthful artist. Moreover, the kind friend had sent him six engravings. These the boy studied with intense pleasure, and soon attempted to imitate. In a retired garret he spread upon the floor these engravings and the canvas upon which he was to copy them, and day after day he stole away and was entirely absorbed in composing a picture from the designs before him. "He had not condescended to copy a single engraving, but had selected the most striking features from a number, and by combining them with wonderful taste and accuracy, had composed a picture as complete in the arrangement of the several parts, and coloring of the whole, as the most skillful artist could have painted under the direction of a finished master."

"Sixty-seven years afterwards, Mr. West had the gratification of seeing this piece in the same room with his sublime painting of 'Christ Rejected,' on which occasion he declared that there were inventive strokes of art in his first juvenile essay, which, with all the knowledge and experience he afterwards acquired, he had never been able to surpass."

The success of these efforts excited the wonder of the primitive people among whom he resided. His parents were Quakers, whose principles were opposed to the cultivation of the fine arts, yet they were proud of the genius of little Benjamin. They allowed him to go to Philadelphia with Mr. Pennington, the friend who had given him the box of paints, and there, for the first time, he saw an oil-painting not his own. At this time Benjamin had read no books but the Bible and a few school books. Profane history and poetry now opened their treasures to him; but little time had he for reading.

The first money that the boy received for artistic labor, was from Dr. Wayne, for some drawings upon poplar boards.

At Lancaster, in Pennsylvania, he made his debut as a portrait painter, and gained not empty praise alone, but substantial remuneration. Here, too, he painted a historical picture. He was employed by one Henry, a gunsmith, to paint the "Death of Socrates." This thrilling incident, which he had never before heard, was read to him by his patron, the gunsmith, and a stalwart workman stood as a model for one of the figures. When Benjamin was about fourteen years old, Dr. Smith, Provost of the College at Philadelphia, visited Lancaster. The boy's pictures were shown to him, and immediately he interested himself in his welfare, and proposed taking him under his own instruction. Gladly did Benjamin avail himself of this opportunity for receiving information. With Dr. Smith he studied history and classical literature, and enjoyed every facility that the city at that time could afford for the pursuit of his favorite art. He remained for two years under the special charge of the Provost, and now at the age of sixteen, it was to be decided whether Benjamin should follow painting as his profession.

John West, and Sarah, his wife, called a meeting of the

Friends in Springfield to decide upon their son's future career. They came to the meeting-house, and gravely deliberated, consulted, and debated upon the subject.

"It was finally concluded that as God had evidently bestowed upon the youth extraordinary genius for the art of painting, it would be presumption in them to attempt to counteract the designs of Omniscience, or to say that these peculiar talents ought not to be cultivated." This conclusion, so liberal, and at the same time so rational, is alike honorable to the youth who was the object of it, and to the assembled elders of a sect whose prejudices and peculiar views were opposed to the occupation to which West seemed destined.

Another meeting was appointed at the house of his father. There, the youthful painter received the blessing of the venerable men and women who were leaders in the Society. In after years, in the midst of his brilliant career, it was a pleasing recollection, and a cause for gratitude, that he had thus received the sanction of the Society to which his family belonged.

After this, Benjamin returned to Philadelphia and diligently pursued his art, as a portrait-painter. "As his mind strengthened and the powers of discrimination increased—as his eyes became open to the beauties of nature, and the power of imitating those beauties increased, the perception of his deficiencies likewise increased. He longed to behold the wonders of art which could at that time only be seen by visiting Italy. This desire stimulated the *industry* and added to the *self-denying frugality* of the virtuous and gifted youth. He looked forward to the time when the product of his industry would enable him to transport himself to the land of the fine arts."

After painting portraits awhile in Philadelphia, at two guineas and a half a head, and five guineas for a half length, Benjamin removed to New-York and there increased his prices.

For eleven months he labored day and night to accomplish the end he had in view. Hearing that a vessel, laden with flour, was to sail from Philadelphia to Leghorn, he was exceedingly anxious to avail himself of this opportunity to reach the land of promise. A Mr. Kelly, of New York, was then sitting to him for his portrait, and Benjamin told him the joyful news. The portrait was speedily finished and ten guineas paid for it. The young painter started for Philadelphia, and was the bearer of a letter from Mr. Kelly. This proved to be an order on his agent for fifty guineas, "to assist the youth in his projected journey and intended studies abroad."

Provost Smith secured the passage of Benjamin West in the vessel, and the son of the owner, Mr. Allen, accompanied him to Leghorn.

Thus everything seemed to conspire for his advancement. He found friends eager to assist him at every step. *Was it not because it was seen by all that every step* was in the right path—that his mind was as deeply imbued with the love of virtue as the love of his art? Such was the character of West through life, and *through life his success was uniform.*

"His father was a man of sense, his mother affectionate and exemplary. He was not spoiled by indulgence, nor soured by thwartings. The most precious part of his education was not entrusted to ignorant and vicious menials; and all who surrounded him were temperate, pure, and happy. The sordid sufferings of poverty were unknown to him, neither was he pampered in the lap of luxury. His physical advantages were great from nature, and the occupations of rural life in childhood tended to strengthen and perfect them. He was taught in the school of realities. He became acquainted with things as they are. His genins was developed by the friends his manners and his virtues gained him. We see the undeviating tribute paid to worth and genius in its ascending progress, in the homely encouragements given by Henry, the gunsmith, the refined and well-directed friendship of Provost Smith, and the frank liberality of the merchants Kelly and Allen."

While West was waiting in Philadelphia for the sailing of the ship, he met with his friend, the gunsmith, and gratefully acknowledged his obligations to Henry for introducing him to the knowledge of history, and for aid in painting the Death of Socrates.

Benjamin West was at the age of twenty-one, when he embarked on his voyage to Italy.

# CHAPTER VII.

## ENCOURAGEMENT.

"Go breathe it in the ear
Of all who doubt and fear,
And say to them, Be of good cheer.—*Longfellow.*

THE bright promise of John Flaxman's childhood, how was it fulfilled in his boyhood ?

Having in his fifteenth year, gained the silver medal at the Royal Academy, Flaxman became in due time, a candidate for the gold one, the reward of the highest merit. He is described at this period, by one who knew him well, as follows :—

"Though little, and apparently weak of body, he was both active and strong—a match for most of his companions in feats of agility, and more than a match in all that regarded genius. He had an earnest, enthusiastic look, and the uncommon brightness of his eyes and fineness of his forehead were not soon to be forgotten. His fellow-students perceived his merit—the grave, the mild and the proud boy was generally respected ; and when he became, in opposition to Engleheart, a candidate for the gold medal, all the probationers and students cried, Flaxman ! Flaxman !

But owing to some misunderstanding or false judgment on the part of the president and members of the Academy, the gold medal was given to his opponent.

Afterwards, in speaking of his disappointment, Flaxman said: "I gave in my model and believed the medal was my own. I knew what Engleheart could do, and did not dread him. I had made up my mind that I was to win, and even invited some friends to cheer themselves at my table till I should return from the Academy with my prize. It was given to Engleheart.—I burst into tears. I determined to redouble my exertions, and put it, if possible, beyond the power of any one to make mistakes for the future."

Flaxman now studied more laboriously than ever, but it became necessary that he should relieve his father as far as possible from the expense of his maintenance. "He was obliged during the day to lay aside his Homer, and seek bread where it could be found." It is as well, perhaps, for men of imaginative genius, that they are obliged to serve a rough apprenticeship in that great workshop, the world; it acquaints them as Milton wished, with seemly arts and affairs, instructs them in the ways of men, and points out the true path to fame if not to fortune. There is some fear indeed of crushing down the spirit by the weight of the yoke; but with minds of great natural vigor the discipline is wholesome. Ben Jonson laid bricks—Burns held the plough—Gifford made shoes, and all were, probably, the better for it. These were tasks less akin to poetry than the models which Flaxman made for the Wedgewoods* were to sculpture. In

* The Wedgewoods still own the porcelain factory where so many beautiful specimens of pottery have been manufactured.

truth, his sketches for those enterprizing and liberal potters were all of a kind with his early studies. They consisted chiefly of small groups in very low relief, the subjects from ancient verse and history. Before those days, the porcelain of England had little external beauty to recommend it in the market. The Etruscan vases and the architectural ornaments of Greece supplied Flaxman with the finest shapes; these he embellished with his own inventions, and a taste for forms of elegance began to be diffused over the land. Rude and unseemly shapes were no longer tolerated. Flaxman loved to allude, even when his name was established, to those humble labors, and since his death, the original models have been eagerly sought after. His labors for the Wedgewoods were so far profitable that they maintained him, but *then he was a frugal person, no lover of strong drink, or of jovial circles, and indeed abstemious in all things, save a hungering and thirsting after knowledge.*

The seclusion to which illness in early youth confined him, had caused him to seek for company in himself, and when grown up to manhood, and full of health and spirits, he still preferred his own studies to public haunts, and casts from the antique, and the poets of Greece and England, to the society of the gay, the witty, and the beautiful. From boyhood to old age he lived the same quiet, simple, secluded sort of life, working by day, and sketching and reading during the evenings. Occasionally, when his daily task was over, he would work at the bust of a friend; but it was his chief delight to make designs from the poets, from the Bible, and from the Pilgrim's Progress. Such attempts, for so he called drawings of no common beauty, were only shown to favorites or to friends. They were arranged in portfolios according to the date of composition, and preserved as memoranda of his early notions, and increasing skill."

The artist is now fairly embarked on the stormy sea of life. Storms he must encounter; calms he must endure; perilous rocks are beneath a smiling surface. His life is, *in a measure*, committed to his own keeping; his true life, that of his spirit, as well as that of his physical nature, and it is his duty to keep both in perfect health. This he cannot do, if he conform his life to what is merely customary and conventional.

The artist's childhood has been full of interest and promise:

> "Trailing clouds of beauty do we come
> From God who is our home:
> Heaven lies about us in our infancy."

Shall it be said that,

> "Shades of the prison-house begin to close
> Upon the growing boy?"

The "vision splendid," that gladdened his early life, must

> "The man perceive it die away,
> And fade into the light of common day?"

Not so—God forbid. Hope and action will keep alive the fire of genius; progress, and a high aim, give it energy and continuity.

There is delight in his work; why then should the artist complain? Having food and raiment, let him be content. He is not seeking wealth—he has a nobler aim. If there be no discordance between his outer and his inner life, no shuddering fear, now that he has come into the thickest of the strife, no paralyzing influence from the scoffs and sneers of men, no stings of conscience—then, onward, onward—

"Heart within and God o'er head."

# CHAPTER VIII.

## SCIENCE.

### GENERAL KNOWLEDGE.

"Genius of any kind, or in any age, is a being of an extremely tender and susceptible nature; it may be stifled in its birth, enervated in its nonage, or curtailed of its fair proportions, *by defect of education*; it has no irresistible tendency towards maturity; it has no indefeasable claim upon immortality. It is not merely a tree, the fruits of which may be sweet or sour according to the measure of its cultivation; it is also not unfrequently a flower which dies or blooms, as it is visited with blight or fostered by the dews and gales of Heaven."—*Henry Nelson Coleridge.*

"A LITTLE learning" is as dangerous a thing for the artist as for the professional man. The artist is not a mere handicraftsman, bound to the labor of the workshop. True, his hands must shape the thoughts which his brain originates, but poor indeed will be his work, without the aid of science. He has to deal with sturdy facts. Ignorance, with regard to facts, may render his productions ridiculous. A poet wrote very prettily of "the little *four*-leafed rose," and we pass lightly over the mistake; but if the painter, in representing the flower, denied it the *five* leaves which Nature has given it, the eye would be offended by the palpable error.

The artist who never saw a palm tree, or a correct delineation of one, would be presumptuous to undertake to ornament his landscape with it; it may not be needful for him to enter into minute detail and finish of each separate leaf and fibre, but he must be so far correct, that the most casual observer would know that it was intended for a palm tree.

The landscape painter, must not only know what vegetation belongs to each country, that he may clothe his landscape in an appropriate garb, but he must understand well, physical geography and geology. If he adorns his landscape with animal life, he must know something of natural history; if with human beings, he must know the customs, manners, costume and characteristics of the people whom he represents; if buildings enter into his composition, he must possess a knowledge of architecture, or he may present the anomaly of a Chinese edifice on a Grecian landscape. In historical painting, he has as wide a field to explore.

The artist must not only paint or sculpture the beautiful, but also the true. The monsters with two heads and five tails, the griffins and dragons, the grinning, long-eared demons, and wide-mouthed satyrs, whose grotesque forms *adorned* ancient edifices, will not be tolerated by modern civilization. The *people* of those olden times were, like children, willing to be amused with efforts of art resembling the literature, of which Jack the Giant Killer, and

> "Heigh! diddle, diddle!
> The cat's in the fiddle;
> The cow jump'd over the moon,"

are fair specimens.

But the people, especially in our own country, are no longer dwarfed in intellect and juvenile in taste. The artist must not calculate upon their ignorance, or their vulgarity. He cannot be a charlatan in art, without detection, for "figures" on canvas, and in marble, "will not lie." Moreover, a man of honest purpose, and of true genius, will not resort to trickery and sham. He will acquire knowledge, that he may maintain self-respect; he will be exact, because he is a lover of truth. Michel Angelo, who was almost idolized in the age in which he lived, and is still considered one of the greatest artists the world has ever produced, was a man of learning and science.

"In the early part of his life, he not only applied himself to sculpture and painting, but to every branch of knowledge connected in any way with those arts, and gave himself so much up to application, that he in a great degree withdrew from society. From this ruling passion—to cultivate his mind—he became habituated to solitude, and happy in his pursuits; he was more content to be alone than in company. When his mind was matured, he attached himself to men of learning and judgment, and in the number of his most intimate friends, were ranked the highest dignitaries of the church, and the most eminent literary characters of his time."

In his professional labors, Michel Angelo continued to study till the end of his life, and was never perfectly satisfied with his own performances. "There is still remaining a design by him, of an old man with a long beard in a child's go-cart, and an hour-glass before him, emblematical of the last stage of life; on a scroll over his head, Anchora Inparo, in Roman capitals, denoting that no state of bodily decay or approximation to death was incompatible with intellectual improvement." He established it as a principle, that to live in credit was enough, if life was virtuously and honorably employed for the good of others and the benefit of posterity; and thus he laid up the most profitable treasure for his old age, and calculated upon its best resources; for he whose wealth serves only to enrich himself, is insulated as life declines, or surrounded by dependents; but he who has cultivated his mind with useful knowledge, and devoted himself to the practice of virtue, makes all mankind interested in the length of his days.

One of Michel Angelo's biographers says, "His knowledge of the anatomy of man and of other animals, was so correct, that those who had all their lives studied it as their profession, hardly understood it so well." When Michel Angelo first visited the dissecting room, he was so disgusted with the offensiveness of the study, that he lost his appetite, and conceiving that his powers of digestjon were impaired; for a time he desisted, but was soon dissatisfied with himself for not being able to do what was every day done by others without inconvenience; he therefore resumed the study, and pursued it to the fullest extent necessary to his profession.

Michel Angelo was as ardently devoted to literature as he was to science. He could repeat, from memory, nearly all the poems of Dante* and Petrarch. *"He also studied with equal attention the sacred writings of the Old and New Testaments."*

A general improvement in taste followed as a consequence from the productions of Michel Angelo. Fuseli says, "if the labors of that wonderful man had perished with him, the change which they effected in the opinions and the works of his cotemporaries would still have entitled him to the first honors of art."

Fuseli, himself, affords another example of profound learning. "He studied the classics in early life, in order to attain a knowledge of what are called the learned languages; taste led him to continue this study, in which he afterwards proved so eminent. He wrote Latin and Greek accurately. He was not ignorant of Hebrew. In modern languages, he was deeply skilled; for he wrote French, Italian, Ger-

* Michel Angelo, besides being a sculptor, architect and painter, was a poet, as the following sonnet on Dante will show:

"He from the world into the blind abyss
Descended and beheld the realms of woe;
Then to the seat of everlasting bliss
And God's own throne, led by his thought sublime,
Alive he soared, and to our nether clime
Bringing a steady light to us below,
Revealed the secrets of eternity.
Ill did his thankless countrymen repay
The fine desire; that which the good and great
So often from the insensate many meet,
That evil guerdon did our Dante find.
But gladly would I, to be such as he,
For his hard exile and calamity,
Forego the happiest fortunes of mankind."

man, and English with equal facility. For the pleasure of reading Lepp's work on "Insects," he gained, late in life, a competent knowledge of Dutch.

Fuseli's acquaintance with English poetry and literature was very extensive; few men recollected more of the text, or understood better the works of Chaucer, Spencer, Shakspeare, Milton and Dryden. How else than by the close study and intense appreciation of a poet, can a painter give life to "*illustrations.*"

Fuseli's knowledge of *history* and *chronology*, was accurate and extensive, and few men understood and remembered better, heathen mythology, and ancient and modern geography. He was not ignorant of *natural history;* but that branch which was cultivated by him with the greatest ardor, was entomology; and in acquiring a knowledge of the habits of insects, he was naturally led into the consideration of their food; hence he was not unlearned in *botany.*

Fuseli was fully sensible of his various acquirements, and sometimes showed, too evidently, that he despised some of his brother artists, "because they were unacquainted with literature and even deficient in orthography.'' He said of them, "I feel humbled, as if I were one of them."

Every one knows, who is acquainted with Art, the powers which Northcote displays in his paintings of the brute creation. When that artist's picture of "Balaam and the Ass" was exhibited at the Macklin Gallery, Northcote asked Fuseli's opinion of its merits; he replied, with more wit than politeness, "My friend, you are an angel at an ass, but an ass at an angel." One of Fuseli's friends, who was fully aware of the faults in Fuseli's character, said to him, with caustic candor like his own, "I hate to see that reptile, Vanity, sliming over the noble qualities of your heart."

Some of his cotemporaries whom he despised, were superior to him in mathematics and the pure physical sciences. To show how important knowledge of all science is to the artist, the following anecdote will be apposite:

In a picture of Lycidas, which Fuseli was executing for Mr. Carrick Moore, he introduced the sun just rising above the horizon, with a full moon, not in opposition to the sun but upon the same side. Mr. Moore attempted to convince Fuseli that the moon never appeared full but when she was diametrically opposite to the sun; but failing to convince him, he advised him to consult his friend, Bonnycastle, the astronomer, on the point. Sometime after, Mr. Moore saw the picture again, and found that the *full moon* was changed to a *crescent.*

As a proof, that an artist required but little knowledge in order to be successful, the example of Hogarth has been adduced; but his biographers, some of them, were such as "considered all as uninformed who had not received a university education; and all human beings as gross in conversation, who were unacquainted with the conventional courtesies of fashionable life."

"If Hogarth showed little bias towards learning, it was because his powerful mind was directed to studies where the knowledge of actual life, in all its varieties, was chiefly essential; where an eye for the sarcastic and ludicrous, and a mind to penetrate motives and weigh character, were worth all the lights of either school or college. But there is no proof that Hogarth was a man gross and uninformed, or that he thought lightly of learning. He was, indeed, a zealous worshiper of knowledge, but he loved to pick the fruit fresh from the tree. Of want of learning no man of Hogarth's pitch of mind will boast. Learning is the *open sesame* which clears up the mysteries of ancient lore, and acquaints us with the lofty souls and social sympathies of the great worthies of the world. Hogarth had not time for everything; he could not, circumstanced as he was, have been both a scholar of eminence, and the first man in a new walk of art. But it is unjust to set him down as despising in the abstract what his own great natural genius enabled him to do without."

In *a measure* to do without; it cannot be doubted that Hogarth would have risen far higher as an artist with the knowledge which circumstances prevented him from attaining. No man should be so presumptuous as to rely entirely upon his own "great natural genius" even though it were equal to that of Michel Angelo, Raffaelle and Thorwaldsen, centered in his single self. Sir Christopher Wren,* the architect was equally celebrated as a mathematician and natural

* Christopher Wren, born in Wiltshire, England, 1632.

philosopher. At the age of thirteen he invented an astronomical instrument, and wrote an account of it, which he dedicated to his father, in Latin. His father, a clergyman of the church of England, educated his talented son till he was fourteen years of age, and then sent him to the university of Oxford.

At the age of sixteen, he had acquired such a knowledge of mathematics and natural philosophy as gave promise of his future distinction.

So skilled was Wren in anatomy, that at the age of fifteen, he was appointed demonstrating assistant to Sir Charles Scarborough. At the age of twenty-five he was elected Professor of Astronomy in Gresham College; and some years before that, he had solved the celebrated problem of Pascal, which had been given as a challenge to English mathematicians; and proposed one to the French mathematicians which was never answered.

He invented a method for projecting solar eclipses; a lunar globe for representing the surface of the moon, with its various mountains and cavities. He wrote a history of the seasons as to temperature, weather, &c., and invented and improved many meteorological instruments. He also made and improved astronomical instruments. He made many improvements in optics. His suggestions and experiments on navigation and practical seamanship were exceedingly ingenious and useful. He invented the art of mezzotinto engraving, and executed all the drawings for Dr. Willis' Treatise on the Brain. Many other useful inventions owe their origin to Christopher Wren.

In 1661, (at the age of twenty-nine,) Wren was elected Professor of Astronomy, at Oxford, and the same year was made Doctor of Laws. While at Oxford he was employed by the king to make drawings of animalculæ seen by the microscope, and Dr. Hook who followed in the footsteps of Dr. Wren in microscopic experiments and drawings says, "I must affirm of Dr. Wren, that since the time of Archimedes, there scarce were met in one man so great a perfection—such a mechanical head and so philosophical a mind."

Sir Isaac Newton, named Sir Christopher Wren, with Wallis and Huygens, as one of the first mathematicians of the age. Yet, he is now better known as the architect of St. Paul's, London. When his mind was directed principally to the art through which he became so famous, he did not entirely abandon his early studies. After London had been nearly destroyed by the great fire, in 1666, Wren drew the plan of a new city, which was submitted to the king, but rejected by the Parliament.

He designed and executed many splendid edifices, but St. Paul's is by far the most famous.

He was President of the Royal Society, and twice sat in Parliament.

By a wretched court intrigue, this ornament of his country was displaced at the age of *ninety* from an office he had held under government, but his religious principles and the nat-

6

ural vivacity of his mind enabled him to bear this unmerited insult.

The last years of his life were spent in perfect serenity, and his faculties were unclouded to the very close of his existence. He was found dead in his chair on the 25th of February, 1723, in the 91st year of his age.

A splendid funeral was decreed to him, and his remains were deposited in the crypt under the southernmost window of St. Paul's. A plain black slab lies above his coffin, but no monument has been reared to his name. On the western jamb of the window of the crypt is a tablet, with the following appropriate and sublime inscription:

Subtus Conditur
Hujus Ecclesiæ et Urbis Conditor
**CH. WREN,**
Qui vixit annos ultra nonaginta
non sibi bono publico.
* Lector, si monumentum quæris
Circumspice.

Sir Joshua Reynolds was the intimate friend of Edmund Burke and Dr. Johnson; and of the benefit, which he derived from intercourse with the latter, he thus speaks in one of his discourses on Art:

"Whatever merit these Discourses may have, must be imputed, in a great measure, to the education I may be said

* Reader, if you ask for his monument, look around.

to have had under Dr. Johnson. I do not mean to say that he contributed even a single sentiment to them, but he qualified me to think justly. No man had like him the art of teaching inferior minds the art of thinking. The observations which he made on poetry, on life, and on every thing about us, I applied to Art—with what success others must judge."

Sir Joshua's advice to Barry was in accordance with his practice. "Whoever," says he, "is resolved to excel in painting, or indeed in any other art, must bring all his mind to bear upon that one object from the moment that he rises till he goes to bed; the effect of every object that meets a painter's eye, may give him a lesson, provided his mind is calm, unembarrassed with other objects, and open to instruction. This general attention, with other studies connected with the art, which must employ the artist in his closet, will be found sufficient to fill up life. Were I in your place, I would consider myself as playing a great game, and never suffer the little malice and envy of my rivals to draw off my attention from the main object."

The whole wide circle of human knowledge is not too wide for the artist; but as he can grasp but a small part during his life, it is all important for him to know *well* what it most concerns him to know. The human figure with all its wonderful machinery cannot be perfectly represented, without an accurate knowledge of anatomy and physiology. *Phrenology* and physiognomy are essential to the painter and sculptor. *Geometry* and *mechanical philosophy* must be understood to enable the artist to draw correctly, and to determine proportions and motion. *Natural philosophy*, more particularly everything concerning light and color, he will find to be indispensable. *Chemistry*, should by no means be neglected.

Every branch of *natural history*, may be useful to him.

*Botany** he can scarcely dispense with.

*Geology* and *geography*, how can he do without them?

*Meteorology*, how can he paint sky and clouds, if in entire ignorance of this branch of science?

He must know the *costume, manners, customs, and peculiarities* of nations, ancient and modern.

*Mental* and *moral philosophy* he cannot dispense with, even if he does not aspire beyond portrait painting.

*"The great masters of Italy, almost without exception, and Titian perhaps more than any, (for he had the highest knowledge of landscape,) are in the constant habit of rendering every detail of their foregrounds with the most laborious botanical fidelity; witness the 'Bacchus and Ariadne,' in which the foreground is occupied with the common blue iris, the aquilegia, and the wild rose; *every stamen* of which latter is given, while the blossoms and leaves of the columbine, (a difficult flower to draw,) have been studied with the most exquisite accuracy. The foreground of Raffaelle's two cartoons—'The Miraculous Draught of Fishes'—'The charge to Peter'—are covered with plants of the common sea colewort, of which the sinuated leaves and clustered blossoms would have exhausted the patience of any other artist, but have appeared worthy of prolonged and thoughtful labor to the great mind of Raffaelle."—*Ruskin*.

## CHAPTER IX.

### HISTORY.

"A significance
Of individual life and passionate ends,
Which overcomes us, gazing."

THE history of the human race is spread out like a boundless ocean, for the noble use of the artist. From that "misty deep," he summons up the mighty spirits of the past, and they come at his bidding, for the pencil and the chisel in his hands are more potent than the wand of Glendower.

The great, the wise, the good, of all ages, when marshalled before him, will not glide by like visionary shadows; his vivifying imagination will clothe them with the habiliments of life. For him they breathe, they think, they "act in the living present." He gives permanency to them in material forms. From ancient profane history, many noble examples of heroism, and of virtue, have been perpetuated by genius. But the Christian Artist has a far nobler "chamber of imagery," from whence to select his inspiring subjects; the history of the Old and New Testament with its inexhaustible treasure.

Sir Joshua Reynolds said of the sculptor, Banks, "His

mind was ever dwelling on subjects worthy of an ancient Greek;" infinitely higher praise would it be to say of an artist, "His mind is ever dwelling on subjects worthy of a Christian." One cause, undoubtedly, of the superiority of the old masters, was their choice of subjects from that sacred source. The Bible was the well-spring of the genius of Michel Angelo, Raffaelle, and Albrecht Durer.

"It is a fact, by no means to be overlooked, that each great master of the old school, not only found full scope for imagination and originality in the sphere of Christian Art, but willingly confining himself within its limits, never grew weary of varying subjects, which might, at first sight, appear to be barren and unfruitful."

"The poets of Greece sung, her philosophers wrote, and her sculptors carved, in the spirit and meaning of their religion—it was addressed chiefly to the eye. In this the heathen differed from the Christian; the former worshiped external beauty, the latter adored the mental and divine." The very architecture became Christian and symbolical in the hands of those old artists. They devoted their grandest and noblest works to their Divine Master.*

* Symbolism was the grand motive and object of the early artists, and it was undoubtedly their intention to make the visible structure of the material church, in all its various parts and proportions, symbolic of the spiritual church of Christ as it exists upon earth, sometimes militant, and sometimes triumphant.—*Schlegel.*

Ruskin, in writing of the Campanile at Florence, of which Giotto was the architect, breaks out into the following glowing and beautiful

They wrought with the spirit of apostles and the zeal of martyrs. The chief end of their labor was, indeed, to "glorify God." Worthy opportunities and glorious themes still remain for lofty spirits to luxuriate in, while pursuing the silent path of deeply rooted, serious, devotional beauty.

What more, then, is needed, to enable the painter to reach the perfection to which he aspires? I reply, that it is most essential, in the first place, that the beautiful truths of the Christian faith and religion, should not be received into the mind as merely lifeless forms, in passive acquiescence to the teachings of others; they must be embraced with an earnest conviction of their truth and reality, and bound up with each individual feeling of the painter's soul. Still, even the influence of devotion is not alone sufficient;

period: The Campanile—that bright, smooth, sunny surface of glowing jasper; those spiral shafts and fairy traceries, so white, so faint, so crystalline, that their slight shapes are hardly traced in darkness on the pallor of the eastern sky; that serene height of mountain alabaster, colored like a morning cloud, and chased like a sea-shell. And if this be, as I believe it, the model and mirror of perfect architecture, is there not something to be learned by looking back to the early life of him who raised it? Not within the walls of Florence, but among the far-away fields of her lilies, was the child trained, who was to raise that headstone of Beauty above the towers of watch and war. Remember all that he became; count the sacred thoughts with which he filled the heart of Italy; ask those who followed him, what they learned at his feet; and when you have numbered his labors, and received their testimony, if it seem to you, that God had verily poured out upon this his servant no common nor restrained portion of his spirit, and that Giotto was indeed a king among the children of men; remember, also, that the legend upon his crown was that of David's: "I took thee from the sheepcote, and from following the sheep."

for however entirely religion may be felt to compensate for our earthly happiness, much more is required to form a painter. I know not how better to designate that other element, without which, mere technical skill and even correct ideas will be unavailing, than by styling it the unborn light of inspiration. It is something quite distinct from fertility of invention, or magic of coloring, rare and valuable as is the latter feature in painting. It is no less distinct from skill in the lofty technicalities of design, and the natural feeling for beauty inherent in some susceptible minds.

This indwelling light of the soul should be recognized in every creation of his pencil, expressive as a spoken word; and in this lies the peculiar vitality of Christian beauty, and the cause of the remarkable difference between classical and Christian Art. Even in the choice of subjects for painting, this ray of inborn inspiration, this divine enthusiasm, must guide and govern the painter's decision.

There are also, it is true, old historical and even mythological subjects, which are not only susceptible of the deeper meaning which the soul demands, but even naturally suggest and give birth to it. Such themes certainly need not be excluded from the circle of Christian Art. It does not, by any means, require an arbitrary restriction to certain exterior forms and given subjects, nor does its beauty depend upon the observance of particular rules, but rather springs from the all-pervading influence of a pure and holy devotion.

But especially should the American artist be intimately acquainted with the history of his own country. He is to be her chronicler for ages yet unborn. He is to send down to the latest generations, the evidence that such men and such deeds have been, though all written records of them may have perished forever.* And in the moral grandeur of American history, he has the highest "motive" for his artistic efforts. He need not stoop to meaner themes, while the daring deeds of our own sages and heroes are yet unportrayed. The Colonies of Roanoke and Plymouth may yet call forth more soul-thrilling sympathy than was ever elicited by Rome or Carthage. The time may—it will come—when that granite obelisk, the Bunker Hill Monument,† will call forth deeper emotions than the pyramids of Egypt, and the mouldering walls of the Capitol far sublimer

*How cold is all history, how lifeless all imagery, compared to that which the living nature writes, and the uncorrupted marble bears. How many pages of doubtful record might we often spare, for a few stones left one upon another. The ambition of the old Babel builders was well directed for this world. There are but two strong conquerors of the forgetfulness of men, Poetry and Architecture; and the latter, in some sort, includes the former, and is mightier in its reality; it is well to have not only what men have thought and felt, but what their hands have handled, and their strength wrought, and their eyes beheld all the days of their life. The day is coming, when we shall confess, that we have learned more of Greece out of the crumbled fragments of her sculpture, than even from her sweet singers or soldier historians.—*Seven Lamps of Architecture.*

†The Bunker Hill Monument was designed by the Architect, Robert Mills, who was born in Charleston, South Carolina. It was, however, originally suggested by Greenough.

sentiments than the Acropolis at Athens. The architects of our country must now have reference to posterity. In this land of freedom from all but wholesome restraint, they can build such edifices as the condition of the country requires, in any style best adapted for the purpose. They have not to choose between the Classical or the Gothic, the Chinese or the Romanesque; but in our architecture, domestic, civil and ecclesiastical, to make a free use of each and all, and, at the same time, be careful that there is fitness, adaptation and national character impressed upon every edifice. It is only by thus doing, that they can be true to themselves and their country, give dignity to the Art, and render their works enduring monuments of our artistic, civil and religious freedom.

# CHAPTER X.

## STUDY OF THE BEST MODELS.

"The artist is born *progressive*, not complete. If, therefore, he feels no inclination to learn from the complete artists of the past and present time, that which he is in want of, to become a proper artist, he will fall short of his own powers, in the false idea of guarding his originality."—*Goethe*.

In the Academy of Fine Arts, in one of our large cities, there is a painting, representing an angel conveying the murdered Abel to Heaven—a stout angel it is, yet the heavy body of Abel seems far more likely to drag an angel down, than to be borne upward by angels' wings. But this is not all; the unfortunate angel is arrayed in a tight-fitting *yoked* night-gown, fastened at the throat with a tawdry bit of jewelry—a turquoise broach! Verily, the artist must have had a meagre wardrobe for the lay-figure* from which he painted the angel! What other model could he have studied? Ancient paintings were frequently grotesque, ridiculous, and for aught we know, painters arrayed their angels after the fashion of their day, in a ball-dress, instead of a yoked night-gown; and far more picturesque would the angel be, in the antique garb, whatever it might have been, than in this modern, every-night fashion. This picture is

* A lay-figure, is the wooden figure, or large jointed-doll, used by artists.

quite on a par with a piece of embroidery once executed at a boarding-school, representing the parting of Hector and Andromache; the sorrowful wife is holding a green, fringed parasol over her head, and the young Astyanax lustily kicking his papa with a pair of new, red morocco boots.

"Study the great works of the great masters forever!" was the enthusiastic advice of Sir Joshua Reynolds to his students. "Study," he continued, "as nearly as you can, in the order, in the manner, on the principles which they studied. Study nature attentively, but always with those masters in your company; consider them as models which you are to imitate, and *at the same time, as rivals which you are to combat.*"

This last consideration would prevent servile imitation and give scope to originality. It is a noble emulation, unlike that between two young artists who are only striving to excel each other.

There is a great deal of twaddle about *self-taught* genius; it has been the boast of many a dunce, puffed up with self-conceit, that he was self-taught. Self-reliant, self-controlled a man may be, but not self-taught. Teaching, as everybody knows, implies instruction that comes from without. For a knowledge of one's own character and capabilities, there must be close introspection; but, after all, the best way of determining both, is by action. If a man believes himself to be a sculptor, or a painter, materials are always at hand by which he can demonstrate the fact. A piece of charcoal or of chalk, would be sufficient for a Michel Angelo to prove withal his aptness for art, and, at the same time, the necessity for his being taught from without. Because a child learns his alphabet in one and the first lesson, does it prove that he has no need of books? Though not exactly a parallel case, it may illustrate the absurdity of those who rely upon their natural quickness of eye, or expertness of hand, or brilliant imagination; who think they are above all teaching as completely as the tree which springs up, bears its leaves, its flowers, and its fruit, because it has an internal principle of life and growth, which will bring it to perfection.

Men boast of being self-taught, when, if they have had other means of teaching and have not employed them, thus to boast, is to glory in their shame. More than one American artist has been ruined by this false notion. Nature-taught, a man may be, when he has elevated himself to the real, earnest contemplation and imitation of her varied charms.

But the study of nature, however loving and constant it may have been, is not sufficient to form the noble artist.

He must learn what others have achieved. He must compare his own crude conceptions with the realized, the embodied conceptions of others. He must exalt the standard of excellence, and keep it ever in advance:

"Perfection ever at kind distance stands,
To tempt the onward chase."

If a young artist has formed a correct estimate of his own power, he will soon make it evident to others. He will, if possible, place himself under the best masters in his own country; he will study the best models, and prepare himself for a wider field of improvement than his own country affords.

By thus proving his own capability at home, he will not be liable to fall into the error of which some artists have been guilty—going abroad before they were sufficiently prepared to apprecaite the *chefs-d'œuvres* of art. By too early entering into the presence of the mighty ones of by-gone times, he may be intimidated—disheartened; unless, indeed, he be gifted with genius equal to that of Correggio, and like him, exclaim with the pride of conscious power, "I, too, am a painter."

But the artist has, not seldom, "to banish preconceived false notions; to dismiss idolized and merely conventional beauties, and strip himself of the absurdities with which he had been bedecking himself from his infancy. He has to rise out of false art into true nature, and this is not to be done in a day." "The man of true genius," says Sir Joshua Reynolds, "instead of spending all his hours, as many artists do while they are at Rome, in measuring statues and copying pictures, soon begins to think for himself, and endeavors to do something like what he sees. I consider general copying a kind of delusive industry; the student satisfies himself with the appearance of doing something; he falls into the dangerous habit of imitating without selecting, and of laboring without any determinate object; as it requires no effort of the mind, he sleeps over his work, and those powers of invention and disposition, which ought particularly to be called out and put in action, lie torpid and lose their energy for want of exercise."

This was not the way in which Sir Joshua himself passed his time at Rome. Northcote, a brother artist, and a friend of Reynolds, thus commends the use he made of his opportunities for improvement: "When arrived in that garden of the world—that great temple of the arts—his time was diligently and judiciously employed in such a manner as might have been expected from one of his talents and virtue. He contemplated, with unwearied attention and ardent zeal, the various beauties which marked the style of different schools and different ages. It was with no common eye, that he beheld the productions of the great masters. He copied and sketched, in the Vatican, such parts of the works of Raphael and Michel Angelo, as he thought would be most conducive to his future excellence, and by his well-directed study, acquired, while he contemplated the best works of the best masters, that grace of thinking, to which he was principally indebted for his subsequent reputation as a portrait painter."

Our own lamented Cole,* not contented with being self-

* The late Thomas Cole was born in England, but in his childhood his father removed to the U. States, and so strong was the painter's attachment to his foster mother, that he was once heard to say, with the

taught, went abroad to study, and writes as follows: "A great deal might be said on the subject of England and Italy. I did not find England so delightful as I had anticipated. The gloom of the climate, the coldness of the artists, together with the kind of art in fashion, threw a tone of melancholy over my mind that lasted for months, even after I had arrived in sunny Italy. *Perhaps my vanity suffered.* I found myself a nameless, noteless individual, in the midst of an immense, selfish multitude. I did not expect much, scarcely anything more than to have an opportunity of studying, and showing some of my pictures in the public exhibitions, and to a few individuals of taste in my own room. *I did study;* but the pictures I sent two seasons, both to the Royal Academy and the British Gallery, were hung in the worst places without exception, so that my acquaintances had difficulty in knowing them.

"At the Gallery of the British Artists I exhibited once, and was better treated. My picture of a 'Tornado in an American Forest' was placed in a good situation, and was praised exceedingly in several of the most fashionable papers. Although, in many respects, I was delighted with the English school of painting, yet on the whole I was disappointed. The standard by which I form my judgment is, beautiful nature; and if I am astray it is on a path which I have taken for truth. In May, 1831, I left Eng-

exaggeration of enthusiasm, "I would give my left hand to identify myself with this country, by being able to say, *I was born here!*"

land for the continent. Modern French painting pleased me even less than English. In landscape they are poor—in portrait, much inferior to the English, and in history, cold and affected. In design they are much superior to the English; but in expression, false.

"The melancholy which I experienced in England continued with me for several months after I had arrived in Italy. I looked upon the beautiful scenery, and knew it to be beautiful but did not feel it to be so. Previous to going to Rome I passed nine months in Florence, which I spent in studying the magnificent collections there, and in painting several pictures, among which was a 'Sunset on the Arno,' and a wild scene for Mr. Gilmor of Baltimore. The 'Arno' was exhibited in the Academy, and seemed to attract attention. I studied and drew from the life at the Academy.

"Florence to me was a delightful residence. The magnificent works of art, the quietness and seclusion in which a man can live, make it a painter's paradise. Indeed, to speak of Italy is to recall the desire to return to it.

"In Rome I was about three months, where I had a studio in the very house in which Claude lived.

"From Rome I went to Naples. I visited Pompeii, Vesuvius, and Pæstum, and at the last place made sketches, from which I have painted, since my return, a view of those magnificent temples.

"I returned to Florence and painted there more pictures

in three months than I have ever done in twice the time before or since. I was in the spirit of it; and I now grieve that information of the sickness of my parents, with their desire for my return, should have broken in upon me. O, that I was there again, and in the same spirit!

"The pictures of the great Italian masters gave me the greatest delight, and I labored to make their principles my own; for these, which have stood the criticism of ages, are produced on principles of truth, and are no abstract notion of the sublime or beautiful. The artists were gifted with a keen perception of the beautiful of nature, and imitated it in simplicity and single-heartedness. They did not sit down, as the modern artist too often does, with a preconceived notion of what is or what ought to be beautiful, but their *beau ideal* was the choicest of nature; they often introduced absurdities and things of bad taste in their pictures, but they were honest—there was no affectation. I do not believe that they theorized as we do; *they loved the beauty that they saw around them—and painted.*"

The beautiful pictures painted by Cole while in Italy, and after his return, demonstrate the advantage he had derived from his intense and loving appreciation of those ancient masters. That he admired his own country, his glowing landscapes prove; and they go far to prove, moreover, his favorite theory, that landscape painting is as high a branch of art as historical painting. He says, "there are certainly fewer good landscape pictures in the world, in proportion to their number, than of historical. In landscape there is a greater variety of objects, textures and phenomena to imitate. It has expression also, not of passion, to be sure, but of sentiment—whether it shall be tranquil or spirit-stirring. Its seasons, sunrise, sunset, the storm, the calm, various kinds of trees, herbage, waters, mountains, skies; and whatever scene is chosen, one spirit pervades the whole—light and darkness tremble in the atmosphere, and each change transmutes. If the talent of Raphael had been applied to landscape, his productions would be as great as those he really did produce."

# CHAPTER XI.

## STUDY OF THE BEST MODELS.

"Houses are built by rule, and commonwealths.
Entice the sun, if that you can,
From his ecliptic line—beckon the sky.
Who lives by rule, then, keeps good company."—*George Herbert.*

In Architecture, a close study of models is still more necessary, than in either painting or sculpture, since Nature here cannot be the only guide. Architecture is not so much an imitative as an inventive art, and in order to know what *can be done,* it is well for every architect to know first what *has been done.**

*Much of the value, both of construction and decoration, in the edifices of men, depend upon our being led by the thing produced or adorned, to some contemplation of the powers of mind concerned in its creation or adornment. I wish the reader to note this especially; we take pleasure, or *should* take pleasure, in architectural construction altogether as the manifestation of an admirable human intelligence; it is not the strength, not the size, not the finish of the work which we are to venerate; rocks are always stronger, mountains always larger, all natural objects more finished; but it is the intelligence, and resolution of man, in overcoming physical difficulty, which are to be the source of our pleasure, and subject of our praise; and again, in decoration or beauty, it is less the actual loveliness of the thing produced, than the choice and invention concerned in the production, which are to delight us; the love and the thoughts of the workman, more than his work; his work must always be imperfect, but his thoughts and affections may be true and deep."—Ruskin. *Stones of Venice.*

From a few simple principles in architecture, are worked out the endless varieties of buildings for man's use. So widely differing are the conditions of the human race, that nearly every individual needs a dwelling just suited to himself. Every community of human beings needs public buildings with the same special application to their religion, civil condition, their amusements and education. Hence arises a boundless field for invention and adaptation. The architect must make himself familiar with all the forms and rules of his art, and then apply them with his own additions and alterations, to suit every individual edifice. He cannot be wholly original, neither should he be cramped and fettered by precedents. He is not obliged to build a Greek edifice in the frozen North, nor Gothic gables in the sunny South. The shady palm, with its broad sheltering leaves, would not be in keeping among the rustling pines of New England, and our graceful elm, with its light foliage, would make but a poor figure amid the luxuriant groves of a tropical clime.

Hence, may be inferred the necessity for a close investigation of the rules and conditions of ancient art; and the causes for the gradual changes which, from time to time, have been developed among different nations.

For the purpose of studying the most celebrated models abroad, Ithiel Town, a native of New England, and, for many years a resident of New Haven, Conn., traveled in Europe for some time, and "examined the works of art with a learned eye and judgment." He collected a "truly magnificent" library, rich in engravings, and as illustrative of Art, "unrivaled," says Dunlap, "by anything of the kind in America; perhaps no private library in Europe is its equal. This splendid library* is open to the inspection of the curious, and freely offered for the instruction of the student."

Our own sculptor, Horatio Greenough, left Harvard College, Cambridge, at the close of his senior year, by permission from the faculty, and went to Rome. There, "his mornings were devoted to making careful drawings of the antique; his afternoons, to modeling from the life some subject of his own composition, which enabled him to exert his invention, and bring into play the practice of the morning; and his evenings, to drawing from the Nudo at the Academy. Having letters to Thorwaldsen, he was enabled to profit by the visits of that distinguished artist." This was in 1825. In consequence of illness, he was obliged to return before the completion of a single year. Scarcely another year had passed, before the enthusiastic young sculptor was again in Italy. He remained for some months at Carrara, "for the purpose of making himself thoroughly acquainted with all the details of preparing and finishing works of sculpture, for which Carrara, being the grand

*At New Haven, most unfortunately, since the death of the lamented architect, this library has been sold and dispersed. Was there no Institution to purchase it?

work-shop of the Italian sculptors, gave him every opportunity. His next remove was to Florence, which he fixed upon as his head-quarters, on account of the advantages in the study of its art, and its healthiness."*

Of the effect produced on the mind of Washington Allston, by the works of the old masters, we may judge by the following extract from his own letters:

"It is needless to say how I was affected by Raffaelle, the greatest master of the affections in art. In beauty he

*A correspondent of the Newark Daily Advertiser, dating at "Florence, January 20th, 1851," writes as follows: "For study and improvement in the fine arts, no city in the world can compare with 'Florence the Fair.'"

"It is most gratifying to know that, in sculpture, our American artists here are prëeminent. The country that gave a discoverer of the New World, degenerated though she be, is rich in the works of the old Titans of Art. Italy hoards these treasures as the miser does his gold—she will not part with them—but, with princely generosity, she opens her bosom to receive and educate the men of genius born on our vigorous soil. As a journal writer, comparisons of our artists' works would be unbecoming, and we confine ourselves to impressions made by frequent visits to the various studios. Greenough has nearly completed his group of the PIONEER, designed for one of the pedestals of the Capitol at Washington. He has been *six* years at work on this. The figures are colossal. A frontier man, in hunting-coat, cap, and fringed leggins, is rescuing his wife and child from the murderous ferocity of a North American Indian. The white man stands nearly erect, with all that *grandeur* of expression which resolution, determination and manly strength can give. He is behind the savage, who appears in the act of smothering both mother and child with his blanket. Grasping him with Herculean strength, his right hand holds the Indian's wrist with a tension and gripe of iron, whilst his left arm, doubled around the Indian's shoulder, has forced the savage on one knee, his face thrown upwards, one hand clutching has often been surpassed, but in grace, the native grace of character—in the expression of intellect, and above all, *sanctity*—he has no equal.

"What particularly struck me in his works, was, the *genuine life* (if I may so call it,) that seemed, without impairing the distinctive character, to pervade them all; for even his humblest figures have a *something* either in air, look or gesture, as if, like living beings under the influence of a master-spirit, they had partaken, in spite of themselves, a portion of the charm which swayed them. This power of infusing one's *own life* into that which is feigned, appears to me the sole prerogative of genius."

a tomahawk, and the other enveloped in the folds of his blanket. The firm, compressed lip of the pioneer, the rugged angry brow, the chin, the *pose* of the head, half-bent over the savage, and the masterly development of muscular strength, render the figure one of surprising excellence. It awes you with the sense of conscious power. It seems to recite the story of our Western progress, the story of the Anglo Saxon superiority over the Red Man. The figure of the Indian, in war-plume and feathers, is admirable in idea of truthfulness. His up-turned, cowering face, acknowledges the power of the pioneer; his whole frame is already relaxed by the (to him) deadly struggle. In front of this group are the wife and child. The mother is seated, clasping the infant to her bosom—her hair, in disarray, floats upon her bared neck and shoulders—her dress falling from her. The fond wife's *horror struck* look, forgetful of self and regardful only of her child, cannot be written. Fear, love, anguish—all are there—the gaze fixed upon the infant, who seems struggling in the mother's arms, unconscious of its danger. The group is a *national, historical* one—it will appeal to the hearts of all Americans—and we have no hesitancy in saying that public opinion at home will pronounce it a sublime conception, grandly executed. The name of Greenough is worthy to stand side by side with Canova's and Thorwaldsen's."

"One must *be* something, in order to *make* something," said Goethe. "Dante seems to us great, but he had the culture of centuries behind him. The house of Rothschild is rich, but it has taken more than one century to accumulate such treasures. All these things lie deeper than is thought. Our artists who imitate the 'old German school,' begin, while weak as men, and uninformed as artists, to copy from nature, and think they become something. They stand *beneath* nature. But he who wishes to do anything great, must be, like the Greeks, so highly cultivated that he will know how to raise up the realities of nature to the height of his own mind; and to realize that, which in nature, whether from internal weakness or external hindrance, has remained an intention merely."

# CHAPTER XII.

## STUDY OF NATURE.

"Nature never did betray
The heart that loved her."—*Wordsworth.*

"Many beauties stand isolated in the world. To discover modes of bringing them together, and thus produce works of art—this is the office of the mind. The flower derives a charm from the insect that rests upon it—the drops of dew that moisten it—the vase from which it draws its last nourishment. There is no bush, no tree, to which the neighborhood of a rock, or spring, does not impart significance, or which does not borrow an added charm from a simple appropriate distance."—*Goethe.*

To advise an artist to study nature seems equivalent to telling him to go about with his eyes open. Yet he, probably, in his boyhood has read the story of "Eyes and no Eyes," and is fully aware that eyes do not always see. True, nature is ever before us, but the sense of the beautiful is not wide awake in all who look upon her loveliness; and in many it seems to be entirely wanting. To study nature, therefore, in all her multitudinous phases, is a very different thing from giving her a casual glance, or going into momentary rhapsodies. There never was a great artist who did not bestow intense study upon natural objects.

The artists who paint landscapes in their studios without ever visiting the waving woods and the living fields, come no nearer to nature on the canvas than they do in their city-bound walks. Their green-baize trees, their solid-lead clouds, their doughy, lumpy foregrounds, prove it. Their zeal, as painters, is not according to knowledge. "He who walks humbly with nature will seldom be in danger of losing sight of Art. He will commonly find in all that is truly great of man's works, something of their original, for which he will regard them with gratitude, and sometimes follow them with respect; while he who takes Art for his authority may entirely lose sight of all that it interprets, and sink at once into the sin of an idolater, and the degradation of a slave."

An admirer of Gainsborough said of him: "Nature sat to him in all her attractive attitudes of beauty, and his pencil traced, with peculiar and matchless felicity, her finest and most delicate lineaments; whether it was the sturdy oak, the twisted eglantine, the mower whetting his scythe, the whistling ploughboy, or the shepherd under the hawthorn in the dale, all came forth equally chaste from his inimitable and fanciful pencil." *

How the poet and painter, Allston, exults in the sublime

* A recent writer confirms the above opinion, as follows: "Gainsborough's power of color is capable of taking rank beside that of Rubens; he is the purest colorist of the whole English school; with him in fact, the *art* of painting did in great part die, and exists not now in Europe. Gainsborough's hand is as light as the sweep of a cloud, as swift as the flash of a sunbeam. His masses are as broad as the first division in heaven of light from darkness; his forms are grand, simple, and ideal; he never loses sight of his picture as a whole. In a word, Gainsborough is an immortal painter; his excellence is based on principles of art, long acknowledged, and facts of nature universally conceded."—*Modern Painters.*

and beautiful of nature! He says in one of his letters, "The impressions left by the sublime scenery of Switzerland, are still fresh to this day. A new world has been opened to me, nor have I met with anything like it since. The scenery of the Appenines is quite of a different character. By the by, I was particularly struck, in this journey, with the truth of Turner's Swiss Scenes—the poetic truth, which none before or since has given, with the exception of my friend Brokeden's magnificent work on the Passes of the Alps. I passed at night and saw the sun rise on the lake Maggiore. Such a sunrise! The giant Alps seemed to rise from their purple beds, and putting on their crowns of gold, to send up a hallelujah almost audible."

The rules of Art are deduced from a study of nature. The ancients did not copy from one model,* and thus only imitate one individual; but they, from a close study of many, worked out what nature, unthwarted, could accomplish—the ideal of the species.†

When Gilbert Stuart,‡ was studying at Somerset House, in the school of the antique, it was proposed by his fellow-students, that each one present should disclose his inten-

* He who depends for all upon his model, should treat no subject but his model.

† Dive in the crowd, meet beauty, follow vigor, compare character, snatch the feature that moves unobserved and the sudden burst of passion, and you are at the school of nature with Lysippus.—*Fuseli.*

‡ Gilbert Charles Stuart, born at Newport, Rhode Island, A. D. 1754.

tions, as to what walk in art, and what master he would follow. The proposal was agreed to. One said he preferred the gigantic Michel Angelo. Another would follow in the steps of the gentle but divine Raffaelle, the prince of painters, and catch, if possible, his art of composition, his expression and profound knowledge of human passion. A third wished to emulate the glow and sunshine of Titian's coloring. Another had determined to keep Rembrandt in his eye, and like him eclipse all other artists in the *chiaro scuro*. Each was enthusiastic in the praise of his favorite school or master. Stuart's opinion being demanded, he said, "I will not follow any master. I wish to find out nature for myself, and see her with *my own eyes*. This appears to me the true road to excellence. Nature may be seen through different media. Rembrandt saw with a different eye from Raffaelle, yet they are both excellent, but for dissimilar qualities. They had nothing in common, but both followed nature. Neither followed in the steps of a master. I will do in that as they did, and only study nature." While he was speaking, Gainsborough came in unobserved by him, and as soon as Stuart ceased, though then a stranger to him, stepped up and patting him on the shoulder said, "That's right, my lad, adhere to that and you'll be an artist,"

Hogarth* considered copying other men's works like "pouring wine out of one vessel into another, there was no increase of quantity, and the flavor of the vintage was liable

* William Hogarth, born in London, A. D. 1697.

to evaporate. He wished to gather in the fruit, press the grapes, and pour out the wine for himself."

Hogarth seldom copied on the spot the object which attracted his notice, but trusted them to a faithful memory. Occasionaly, he made a sketch on his thumb-nail of any remarkable form, face, or feature which came in his way, and thus carried it home to transfer to his sketch-book, or canvas.

He says, "Instead of burthening the memory with musty rules or tiring the eye with copying dry or damaged pictures, I have ever found studying from nature the shortest and safest way of obtaining knowledge of my art. Nature is simple, plain, and true, in all her works, and those who strictly adhere to her laws, and closely attend to her appearances in all their infinite varieties, are guarded against any prejudicial bias from truth."

"Every master-spirit," says Allan Cunningham, "every master-spirit that appears on the earth goes to work in his own peculiar way; and though the structures which he raises are founded in nature, yet they differ in the exterior effect and internal arrangement from what has preceded them, as the Gothic architecture differs from the Grecian. The rules for composition are overthrown by another who forms his own laws; and these again are swept away by the next succeeding spirit, as readily as a wave of the sea obliterates words written on the sands. Men, whose feelings were imbued with nature, wrought by a kind of instinctive inspiration in the right way, when they executed those statues and paintings which continue to astonish the earth." What is the merit of a painter? Ask the biographer of Hogarth:* To represent life; to give us an image of man; to exhibit the workings of his heart; to record the good and evil of his nature; to set in motion before us the very beings with whom earth is peopled; to shake us with mirth; to sadden us with woful reflection; to please us with natural grouping, vivid action, and vigorous coloring—if he that has done so be not a painter who will show us one? I claim a signification, as wide for the word *painter* as for the word *poet*. But there seems a disposition to limit the former to those who have been formed under some peculiar course of study, and produce works in the fashion of such and such great masters. This I take to be mere pedantry; as well might all men be excluded from the rank of poets, who had not composed epics, dramas, odes, or elegies, according to the rules of the Greeks.

Where on the wide earth could a painter better study nature than in our own broad land? Our transparent sky—our placid lakes—our mountain torrents—our glorious rivers, with their magnificent waterfalls—hills and valleys, clothed with varied living verdure—our sea-beat cliffs, and cloud-piercing mountains—where could the landscape painter find more noble inspiration?

The varieties of human beings and modes of human life

* Allan Cunningham.

here offered to his study, are such as no other country can afford. Men of every race and every clime have here been rolled together and amalgamated, like the "pudding-stone" of the Potomac, in the amalgam of our civil goverment, without destroying their strongly-marked individual characters. The sunny South offers her glowing beauty, and the cooler North her delicate loveliness; the teeming West her ruddy denizens of the forest, and the wave-washed East the refined and elegant habitant of cities.

Here,are nooks and corners where civilization has scarcely yet sent a single ray; there,rural homes, smiling with Arcadian peace, simplicity and loveliness. Here,is border life, in which Salvator Rosa might have revelled—there, a Swiss hamlet where the peasantry retain their picturesque costume. Here, are stalwart soldiers encamped on the wide prairie—there,pioneers felling their way through a primeval forest. Nature is here lavish in her gifts, and already have American artists demonstrated that they have been mindful of her teachings, and grateful for her boundless generosity.

In the course of time landscape gardening will take a high place among the Fine Arts in our country. "All just and solid pleasure," said the poet Wordsworth, "all just and solid pleasure of natural objects rests upon two pillars, God and man. Laying out grounds as it is called, may be considered as a liberal art, in some sort like poetry and painting, and its object, like that of all the liberal arts, is, or ought to be, to move the affections under the control of good sense;

that is of the best and wisest; but speaking with more precision, it is to assist nature in moving the affections, and surely, as I have said, the affections of those who have the deepest perception of the beauty of nature; who have the most valuable feelings, that is, the most permanent, the most ennobling connected with nature and human life. No liberal art aims merely at the gratification of an individual, or a class. The painter or the poet is degraded in proportion as he does so; the true servants of the Arts pay homage to the human kind as impersonated in unwarped and enlightened minds. If this be so when we are merely putting together words or colors, how much more ought the feeling to prevail when we are in the midst of the realities of things; of the beauty and harmony, of the joy and happiness of loving creatures; of men and children, of birds and beasts; of hills and streams, and trees and flowers; with the changes of night and day, evening and morning, summer and winter, and all their unwearied actions, and energies, as benign in the spirit that animates them, as they are beautiful and grand in that form of clothing which is given them for the delight of our senses."

# CHAPTER XIII.

## POETRY.

"All noble ornament is the expression of man's delight in God's work."—*Ruskin*.

"Here on all the shining boughs,
Knowledge fair and useful grows;
On the same young flowery tree
All the seasons you may see;
Nations in the bloom of light,
Just disclosing to the sight;
Here are thoughts of larger growth;
Ripening into solid truth;
Fruits refined of noble taste;
Seraphs feed on such repast.
Here, in a green and shady grove
Streams of pleasure mixed with love;
There beneath the smiling skies
Hills of contemplation rise;
Now upon some shining top
Angels light, and call me up;
I rejoice to raise my feet,
Both rejoice when there we meet."

FROM the time of Phidias and Apelles down to our own day, the poet has given the stimulus to all other artists; he has done more; he has supplied "airy" shapes to which they have given a "local habitation." The song of the poet has inspired the musician, the descriptions of the poet have been embodied in living colors, breathed in marble, and been perpetuated in glorious edifices. Does a sculptor seek a motive for his chisel? The ideal characters which genius has created, give scope to his imagination. The legions of statues which thronged the temples, the houses, the streets and the highways of ancient Greece, had, nearly all of them, their prototypes in the Iliad, and the Odyssey of Homer. Down the vista of ages, even to the present, is perpetuated the long line of gods, goddesses, heroes, sages, and beautiful women, the progeny of his mighty genius.*

Shakspeare† has peopled the realm of painting with his own creations. It would be amusing to study the statistics of Picturedom, and learn how many "illustrations" have been made from Shakspeare and Milton, Tasso and Dante.

* The Iliad is a storehouse of rude and imperfect art, as it is a mirror of consummate nature. "The elements of all the arts," says Quintilian, "are found in Homer; and, indeed, there is hardly a department of human labor and knowledge, which, directly or indirectly, according to the measure of the times, is not introduced in the Iliad. The geography of Greece, and of the coasts of Asia Minor, is exact; the acquaintance with Egypt and Phœnecia, obvious; the wind, the waves, and the foam of the ocean, the motion, the sound, and the tackle of the ship, are described with the familiarity and the fondness of a frequent mariner. In surgery, in agriculture of many kinds, in *architecture*, in fortification, in smiths' and carpenters' work, the attainments of the age are technically displayed."—*H. N. Coleridge.*

Each individual of Homer forms a class, and is circumscribed by one quality of heroic power. The height, the strength, the giant-stride and supercilious air of Ajax; the courage, the impetuosity, the never-failing aim, the never-bloodless stroke of Diomedes; the presence of mind, the powerful agility of Ulysses; the velocity of the lesser Ajax; Agamemnon's sense of prerogative and domineering spirit, etc., etc.—*Fuseli.*

† The greatest poets that have ever lived, have, without exception, been among the wisest men of their times. I say wisest, because the word learned is often misunderstood; the wisdom of the poet may include more or less of book-learning, as it may happen; in the present age it must include some certainly; but the knowledge of the

However largely ideality may be developed in the artist, he will not content himself with the creations of his own imagination. He will revel among the poets, not for self-pleasing alone, but to widen his field of mental vision, and to exalt and beautify, through the medium of their conceptions, nature herself.

Eckermann said of Goethe, "His works are for the artists whose mind they enlighten as to general principles, and whom they teach what subjects are suited to works of art; what he should use, and what leave aside. All those who are engaged in science or art, may be guests at his richly-provided table, and in their works show plainly that they have drawn from a great general source of light and life."

Indeed, painting and sculpture are only material exponents of poetry. The artist is a poet; if he sees in the

mind and its powers, of the passions and their springs, the love and study of the beautiful forms of the visible creation—this it is which alone can teach a man to think in sympathy with the great body of his fellow-creatures, and enable him to draw back the veil which different manners and various customs have spread over the unchangeable essence of humanity. In this sense it is most true that Homer, and Dante, and Milton, were learned in an extraordinary degree; but more than all, that Shakspeare was the most learned man that ever lived and was not directly inspired by Heaven.—*Coleridge.*

"On the tip of his subduing tongue
All kinds of arguments and questions deep,
All replication prompt, and reason strong,
For his advantage still did wake and sleep,
To make the weeper laugh, the laugher weep;
He had the dialect and different skill,
Catching all passions in his craft of will,
That he doth in the general bosom reign
Of young, of old."

visible forms around him, instinct with life and beauty, the symbols of higher and nobler things, and lifts up his soul through them to the Almighty Creator—or in the oft-quoted words of the poet—

> "Looks through nature up to nature's God,"

with reverence and love, and then attempts to portray the images in his own glowing mind—is he not a poet? His fervid imagination may create *visible* imagery in marble and on canvas; or, through language that "breathes" and "burns," he may present the same imagery.

"A great painter and a great poet must alike be formed by study and instruction. The elementary course of their instruction is parallel. Expansion is given to the same powers of mind; the same models are held up to their admiration; similar passions are to be delineated by each, and both are intent to catch the living features. It is only in the application of principles to practice, that their paths diverge. Versification and coloring, plot and perspective, are the mechanical branches which constitute the difference of their arts."

When the poet, Dante, was in exile at Ravenna, he heard that his distinguished fellow-citizen, Giotto, was then studying at Ferrara, and sent to invite him to come and join him. The painter went, and there a friendship was formed between these extraordinary men, which served to soothe the grief and bitter feelings of the poet's mind.

While at Florence, in the year 1322, tidings were received by Giotto of the death of his friend, the celebrated poet. Giotto deeply felt the loss of his friend, and some of the next works he executed owed their chief excellence to former conversations with Dante, which he now recalled.

Many artists have adopted both modes of portraying their exquisite perceptions of the beautiful in nature, of the noble in sentiment, the delicate and sublime in character.

Allston was as truly a poet, as he was a painter. What painter could more vividly present a scene through the medium of drawing and colors, than Allston has done in the following passage? "We made Boston harbor on a clear evening in October. It was an evening to remember! The wind fell and left our ship almost stationary on a long, low swell, as smooth as glass, and *undulating, under one of our gorgeous autumnal skies, like a prairie of amber.* The moon looked down upon us like a living thing, as if to bid us welcome," etc. "I was in the very waters," he continues, with a burst of patriotic feeling, "which the gallant Constitution had first broken; whose building I saw when at college, and whose 'slaughter-breaking brass,' to use a quotation from worthy Cotton Mather's Magnalia, but now 'grew hot and spoke' her name among the nations." Allston has somewhere said, that unless the spectator possess the imaginative faculty, the works of some of the great masters "will have little more meaning to him than a calico counterpane."

His own vivid imagination gave life and reality to pictures of all kinds. He says, "I am by nature a *wide liker*. I cannot honestly turn up my nose even at a piece of still life, since, if well done, it gives me pleasure. A picture of a totally different kind, by Ludovico Carracci, took great hold on me. The subject was the body of the Virgin, borne for interment by four apostles. The figures are colossal, the tone dark, and of tremendous depth of color. It seemed, as I looked at it, *as if the ground shook under their tread, and the air were darkened by their grief*."

"To no other man whom I have known," said Allston, "do I owe so much, *intellectually*, as to Mr. Coleridge, with whom I became acquainted in Rome, and who has honored me with his friendship for more than five and twenty years. He used to call Rome the *silent* city; but I never could think of it as such, while with him; for, meet him when or where I would, the fountain of his mind was never dry, but like the far-reaching aqueducts that once supplied this mistress of the world, its living stream seemed specially to flow for every classic ruin over which we wandered. When I recall some of our walks under the pines of the Villa Borghese, I am almost tempted to dream that I had once listened to Plato, in the groves of the Academy. It was there he taught me this golden rule: *never to judge of any work of art by its defects;* a rule as wise as benevolent, and one that while it has spared me much pain, has widened my sphere of pleasure.

A volume of poems, by Allston, was published as early as 1813, in London.

Eckermann, in his conversations with Goethe, tells us that the poet showed a landscape painted by Rubens, which was painted with such truth and fidelity, that he remarked, "Rubens must have copied the picture from nature." "By no means," said Goethe; "so perfect a picture is never seen in nature. We are indebted for its composition, to the poetic mind of the painter; but the great Rubens had such an extraordinary memory, that he carried all nature in his head, and she was always at his command in the minutest particulars. Thence comes such truth in the whole and in parts, that we think it must be a copy from nature. No such landscapes are painted now-a-days. This way of feeling and seeing nature no longer exists. Our painters are wanting in poetry."

The only true fountain of beauty, is *feeling.* It is *feeling* which reveals to us true ideas and correct intentions, and gives that indefinable charm, never to be conveyed in words, but which the hand of the artist, *guided by the poet's soul alone,* can diffuse throughout all his works. From religious feeling, love, and devotion, arose the silent inborn inspiration of the old masters; few, indeed, now seek their hallowed inspiration, or tread the paths by which alone they could attain it, or emulate that earnest endeavor to work out the principle of serious and noble philosophy, which is discoverable in the works of Durer and Leonardo da Vinci.

Vain will be our effort to recall the genius of art, until we summon to our aid the Christian philosophy founded on religion. Still, if young artists deem this road too distant or too difficult of attainment, let them at least study deeply the principles of poetry, in which the same spirit ever breathes and moves. Not so much the poetry of the Greeks, as Shakspeare, the best Italian and Spanish dramatists, and those, also, of the old German poems which are most accessible; and next, such modern productions as are dictated by the spirit of romance. These should be the constant companions of the youthful artist; they will lead him back to the fairy-land of old romantic days, chasing from his eyes the prosaic mist, engendered by imitation of the pagan antique, and the unsound babble of conventional art. Still, every effort will be fruitless, unless the painter be endowed with earnest religious feeling, genuine devotion and immortal faith.*

Goethe advised a friend to make a capital that would be permanently useful, by the study of the English and literature. The same recommendation he might have offered to an artist: "You have not been able greatly to avail yourself of the ancient languages during your youth; seek now a strong hold in the literature of so able a nation as the English. These fifty years I have been busy with the English language and literature. But," said he, addressing a young Englishman, "you do well to come to us and learn our lan-

* Schlegel.

guage; for not only does our own literature merit attention, but no one can deny that he who knows German can dispense with many other languages. French, indeed, cannot be dispensed with; for it is the language of conversation, and essential to comfort in traveling, as every body understands it, and in all countries it serves you instead of an interpreter. But as for Greek, Latin, Italian, and Spanish, we can read the best works of those nations in excellent translations, and unless we have some particular object in view, we may well dispense with spending much time upon the toilsome study of their languages. You get a great deal from a good translation."

The spirit of poetry never dies; even in this mechanical age it is rife. Earth, sky, and ocean send up a perpetual hymn. The "good old days," of which men delight to speak, were no better than the present. So sings the poet Milnes:

"I know not that the men of old
Were better than men now;
Of heart more kind, of hand more bold,
Of more ingenuous brow;
I heed not those who pine perforce
A ghost of Time to raise,
As if they could check the course
Of these appointed days."

No! glorious things in Art are yet to be accomplished, before which all the noble works that hitherto have delighted mankind, shall pale their ineffectual fires; for

Past and Future are the wings
On whose support harmoniously conjoined
Moves the great spirit of Human Knowledge.

## CHAPTER XIV.

### PORTRAIT PAINTING.

"Portrait painting is one of the ministers of vanity, and vanity is a munificent patroness. Historical painting seeks to revive the memory of the dead, and the dead are very indifferent paymasters. Students who confine their studies to the works of the dead need never hope to live themselves."—*Hogarth.*

IN the United States, as in other countries, almost every painter commences with portraits, and until his reputation is established, and perhaps for the greater part of his life, he must depend upon this branch of his art for support. To be popular and successful as a portrait painter, requires much artistic skill and talent, a deep insight to human character, and the capability of adaptation to endless varieties of human beings.

The husband of the celebrated Amelia Opie was a painter of portraits, though he altogether preferred historical painting. In vindicating her husband from the accusation of "speaking his mind" to his sitters, she says: "Of all employments portrait painting is, perhaps, the most painful and trying to a man of pride and sensibility, and the most irritating to an irritable man. To hear beauties and merits in a portrait stigmatized as deformities and blemishes—to have high lights taken for white spots, and dark effective shadows for the dirty appearance of a snuff taker—to witness discontent in the bystanders, because the painting does not exhibit the sweet smile of the sitter, though it is certain that a smile on canvas often looks like the grin of idiocy, while a laughing eye, if the artist attempts to copy it, as unavoidably assumes the disgusting resemblance of progressive intoxication. Sitters, themselves, Mr. Opie rarely found troublesome; but *persons of worship*, as he called them, that is, persons of great consequence, either from talent, rank, or widely spreading connections, are sometimes attended by others, whose aim is to endeavor to please the great man, or woman, by flattery, wholly at the expense of the poor artist, and to minister sweet food to the palate of the patron, regardless though it be as wormwood to that of the painter. Hence arises an eulogy on the beauties and perfections of the person painted, and regrets that they are so inadequately rendered by the person painting; while frivolous objection succeeds to frivolous objection, and impossibilities are expected and required. I have too frequently witnessed this, and my temper and patience have often been on the point of deserting me, while Mr. Opie's had not, apparently, undergone the slightest alteration, a strong proof that he possessed some of that self-command which is one of the requisites of good breeding."

Opie painted a portrait of Charles Fox, which was hung up in the exhibition room of the Academy. A dinner was given in the exhibition room, at which Fox sat opposite to Opie; he remembered that he had given less time to the painter than he requested, and said, across the table: "There, Mr. Opie, you see I was right; everybody thinks it could not be better. Now, if I had minded you, and consented to sit again, you most probably would have spoiled the picture."

While this far-famed portrait was in progress, Opie became alarmed for his success; he was distracted by a multitude of hints, which friends, who came in swarms, dropped, regarding the expression, the posture, and the handling. Fox was amused with the variety of opinions, and kindly whispered to Opie, "Don't mind what these people say—you must know better than they do."

It is said that there was a want of grace and softness in Opie's female heads till after his marriage with Amelia Opie. When he exhibited some portraits soon after that event, one of his brother artists said to him, "Opie, we never saw anything like this in you before; this must be owing to your wife." It is altogether probable that the artist had divined the true cause of Opie's improvement.

The industry of Opie was indefatigable. "He was always in his painting room by half past eight in winter, and by eight o'clock in summer, and there he generally remained, closely engaged in painting, till half past four in winter, and till five in summer. He did not suffer his exertions to be paralyzed by neglect, the most unexpected, nor by disappointment, the most undeserved."

Hogarth was a man of rough address, unpolished manners, and encumbered with the dangerous reputation of a *satirist.** He was unacquainted with the art of charming a peer into a patron, by putting him into raptures with his own good looks. There were other drawbacks. The calm, contemplative look, the elegance of form without the grace of action, and motionless repose, approaching to slumber, were not for him, whose strength lay in kindling figures into life, and tossing them into business. A collection of isolated lords and ladies, each looking more lazily into vacancy than the other, compared with historical pictures, are as recruits drawn up in line and put into position by the drill-sergeant, compared to soldiers engaged in the tumult of battle, animated with high passions, and determined to do or die.

Compared with the productions of the great masters of the art of portraiture, those of Hogarth are alike distinguished for their vigorous coarseness and their literal nature. Ladies accustomed to come from the hands of men

* This propensity to satire is a dangerous one. As Giotto was completing a picture for the king of Naples, who spent many hours in the painter's studio, the monarch observed in jest: "Now, Giotto, I should like you to paint me something on a larger scale; for instance, my own kingdom." Giotto soon after presented the king with the painting of an ass, suffering under a heavy bastinado. Instead of resenting the blows, the beast was busy with his nose and feet at another bunch of rods, larger than that he felt upon his back, as if desirous of making an exchange. On both the instruments of chastisement were painted the royal crown and sceptre. Whether or not the king thought the painter carried the jest too far, it is certain Giotto very soon after left Naples.

practiced in professional flattery, with the airs of goddesses, and sometimes with the name, would ill endure such a plain-spoken mirror as Hogarth's. *He was, moreover, no picker of pleasant words.* These circumstances were not very likely, either to augment the number of Hogarth's sitters, or to cheat him into good humor with an originally uncongenial task. How striking the contrast between Hogarth and his more popular rival, Sir Joshua Reynolds.

The portraits of Reynolds were equally numerous and excellent, and all who have written of their merits, have swelled their eulogiums by comparing them with the simplicity of Titian, the vigor of Rembrandt, and the elegance and delicacy of Vandyke. Certainly, in character and expression, and in manly ease, he has never been surpassed. He is always equal—always natural—graceful—unaffected. His boldness of posture, and his singular freedom of coloring, are so supported by all the grace of art—by all the sorcery of skill—that they appear natural and noble. Over the meanest head he sheds the halo of dignity; his men are all nobleness; his women all loveliness, and his children all simplicity; *yet they are all like the living originals.* He had the singular art of summoning the mind into the face, and making sentiment mingle in the portrait. He could completely dismiss all his preconceived notions of academic beauty from his mind, be dead to the past, and living only to the present; and enter into the character of the reigning beauty of the hour, with a truth and a happiness next to magical.

Burke, in pronouncing an eulogium upon his friend, Sir Joshua, said: "In full affluence of foreign and domestic fame, admired by the expert in art and by the learned in science, courted by the great, caressed by sovereign powers, and celebrated by distinguished poets, his native modesty never forsook him, even on surprise or provocation; nor was the least degree of arrogance or assumption, visible to the most scrutinizing eye, in any part of his conduct or discourse."

Reynolds had been warned by the surly, intractable, sarcastic spirit of Hogarth, which prevented his success in portraiture, and resolved to woo the smiles of fortune in a very different manner.

He who would succeed as a portrait painter must practice the patience and the courtesy of a fine lady's physician. It is not enough to put the sitter into a suitable posture, he must also, by conversation, move him into a suitable mood of mind, and an ease—a natural, unembarrassed ease of expression. He has, moreover, to keep him thus throughout the whole of a tedious operation.

Gainsborough had none of the patience and courtesy which rendered Reynolds so eminently successful. A certain lord went to Gainsborough to sit for his portrait. That all might be worthy of his station, the nobleman had put on a new suit of clothes, richly laced, with a well-powdered wig. Down he sat, and put on a practiced look of such importance and prettiness, that the artist, who was no flatterer, either with tongue or pencil, began to laugh, and was heard to mutter, "This will never do." The patient having composed himself in conformity with his station, said: "Now, sir, I beg you will not overlook the dimple on my chin." "Confound the dimple on your chin," said Gainsborugh; "I shall neither paint the one nor the other." And he laid down his brushes and refused to resume them.

The sculptor, Nollekens, seems to have treated his "patients" in a very different manner. He was a blunt, honest man, with much oddity and simplicity of manner. But these traits rendered him at times quite amusing, particularly to the ladies, who sat to him for their busts.

"While Nollekens was modeling the head of a lady of rank, she forgot herself, changed her position and looked more loftily than he wished: "Don't look so *scorney*," said the sculptor, modeling all the while, "else you will spoil my bust—and you are a very fine woman; I think it will make one of my very best busts."

Another time, he said to a lady who had a serious squint, "Look for a minute the other way, for then I shall get rid of that slight shyness in your eye, which, though not ungraceful in life is unusual in art."

On another occasion, a lady with some impatience in her nature was sitting for a portrait; every minute she changed her position, and with every change of position put on a change of expression; his patience gave way: "La, woman!" exclaimed the unceremonious sculptor, "What matter how handsome you are if you wont sit still till I model you." The lady smiled, and sat ever afterwards like a lay-figure.*

The facetious Gilbert Stuart, on one occasion, exclaimed: "What a business is this of a portrait painter! You bring him a *potato*, and expect he will paint you a *pear*."

The portrait painter must maintain his own self-respect without pride, and his modesty without self-abasement. He may neither despise the humble, nor cringe to the rich and powerful. The artist's studio is oftentimes considered a privileged place for gossipping. Uundoubtedly, there are great temptations to gossip for the amusement of sitters; but remember that gossip needs to be made racy; and, too frequently, the condiment for that purpose is downright scandal. The artist, of course, sees a great deal that is amusing and ludicrous, and to keep his sitters in good humour he will be tempted to draw upon his memory for ridiculous stories, which will serve well for that purpose. The sitters who are thus amused will not feel very comfortable when they consider that they are in turn to be served up to others in the same way.

Another temptation to the artist, arising from the nature of his profession, is too great a love of society; the society of the gay, the idle and the dissipated. Frivolous society, which will lower the tone of his mind and character—dissipated society, which will drag him down to the depths of ruin.

* Cunningham.

He needs relaxation, and instead of seeking it in a ramble in the country, or a ride on horseback, by which both the physical and mental system would be invigorated, he flies to the crowded assembly, the pernicious club, or the bar-room. The habit of "entertaining boon companions, and setting the table in a roar," totally unfits a man for an artist. He requires a steady hand and a steady head. One who knew better how to moralize than to practice, a well-known portrait painter, expatiated to another artist on two pictures he intended to paint, as follows:

"In one," said he, "I show the effects of bad habits and strong liquors. I will paint a farm-house with everything around it going, or gone to ruin; fences down—gates broken or unhinged—windows shattered, and old hats and petticoats for panes of glass—the man of the house in rags, and bloated, reeling home from a tavern—his wife sallow, dispirited and sick, the children neglected, filthy, and crying for bread. In the other picture, I will exhibit the effects of industry and temperance on another farm-house and its inmates. The house and fences neat and painted white; all serene around, and in the distance a golden harvest. The white house, shaded by luxuriant fruit trees, the man, full of health and vigor, having returned from the field, has his blooming children around him and is plucking cherries for them, while his wife, full of health, and smiling with content, looks at him whom she loves, and invites him in to his meal. In short, such a place as the abode of temperance must be."

"By this time," says the brother artist, "we had arrived at the abode of the painter who could conceive and describe these scenes, and a commentary on the text was given. In the front room was an easel, a pallet and brushes, with the paint dried upon them. Two or three bad unfinished portraits on the floor, confused furniture in scant quantity, and a little dirty boy. The painter threw open a door and invited me into a back apartment. It was small; on one side was a bed, and on the other a pile of wood. Opposite to the door was a kind of cupboard. The centre of the room was occupied by a table with bottles and glasses. He opened the cupboard and took out a decanter of brandy, a pitcher of water, and two tumblers, for which he found room on the table. 'Come,' said he, 'drink.' 'No,' I replied 'I belong to the *white house.*' 'Well, well,' said he, filling a tumbler more than half full of brandy, 'if you will not drink you shall see me drink,' and adding some water, swallowed the whole."

The result of such conduct was such as might have been anticipated. At the age of fifty-four, an age at which men with half the vigor that he had been blessed with by nature, are strong in body, and more strong in mind than at earlier periods, his mind and body were destroyed. The excellent artist could not paint—the tongue which delighted the hearer was paralyzed—the memory which furnished rich ideas for a rich imagination to combine was no more. With a frame of iron and constitution of steel, with a mind to contrive and a hand to execute, nature had endowed this extraordinary man; but the good gifts were misused, the blessing of health and strength counteracted by poisons, and the name of the unfortunate artist, a man of great talents and kind disposition, can only be used "to point a moral."

# CHAPTER XV.

## MORALITY.

"Who is the honest man?
He that doth still and strongly good pursue,
To God, his neighbor and himself, most true,
Whom neither force nor frowning can
Unpin, or wrench from giving all their due.

"Who never melts or thaws
At close temptations! When the day is done,
His goodness sets not; but in dark can run.
The sun to others writeth laws,
And is their virtue; virtue is his sun."—*George Herbert.*

To resist the *peculiar* temptations which haunt his footsteps, an artist must possess *fixed principles,* and great *decision* of *character* to maintain those principles. He is tempted to flatter; flattery leads to deceit and falsehood.

"Do not let us lie at all," says the eloquent Ruskin; "do not think of one falsity as harmless, and another as slight, and another as unintended. Cast them all aside; they may be light and accidental, but they are an ugly soot from the smoke of the pit, for all that; and it is better that our hearts should be swept clean of them. Speaking truth is like writing fair, and comes only by practice; it is less a matter of will than of habit, and I doubt if any occasion can be trivial which permits the practice and formation of such a habit. To speak and act truth with constancy and precision, is nearly as difficult, and perhaps as meritorious, as to speak it under intimidation and penalty. And seeing that of all sin, there is, perhaps, no one more flatly opposed to the Almighty, no one more wanting in virtue than this of lying, it is surely a strange insolence to fall into the foulness of it on slight, or on no temptation, and surely becoming an honorable man to resolve that whatever semblances or fallacies the necessary course of his life may compel him to bear or to believe, none shall disturb the serenity of his voluntary actions. I would have the spirit of Truth clear in the hearts of our artists."

*Method* and *punctuality*, are essential requisites for a successful portrait painter.

Sir Joshua Reynolds gives an account of the economy of his studies and the distribution of his time, during the most lucrative part of his professional career, which is both curious and instructive:

"It was his practice to keep all the prints engraved from his portraits, together with his sketches, in a large portfolio; these he submitted to his sitters, and whatever position they selected, he immediately proceeded to copy it upon his canvas, and paint the likeness to correspond. He received six sitters daily, who appeared in their turns; and he kept regular lists of those who sat, and of those who were waiting until a finished portrait should open a vacancy for their admission. He painted them as they stood on his list. Of lounging visitors he had a great abhorrence, and, as he reckoned up the fruits of his labors, said, 'those idle people do not consider that my time is worth five guineas an hour.' He rose early, breakfasted at nine, entered his study at ten, examined designs or touched unfinished portraits, till eleven brought a sitter; painted till four, then dressed and gave the evening to company.

"'Notwithstanding his professional diligence, and the time which he was compelled to yield to the attachment of friends and the curiosity of strangers, he found leisure to study, and to note down many useful remarks concerning his art. He had a decided aversion to loquacious artists, and spoke little himself while he was busied at his easel. When artists love to be admired for what they say, they will have less desire to be admired for what they paint. Dr. Johnson, when questioned by Boswell on the merit of portraits, said, 'Sir, their chief excellence is being like—I would have them in the dress of their times, to preserve the accuracy of history; truth, sir, is of the greatest value in these things.' To give the exact form and pressure of the man, and animate him with his natural portion of intellect and no more, requires a skillful hand, and a head which the love of flattering is unable to seduce from the practice of truth; to bestow proper expression, just character, and unstudied ease, is infinitely difficult. Reynolds said he could teach any boy, whom chance might throw in his way, to paint a likeness. To paint like Velasquez is another thing. He did at once and with ease, what we cannot accomplish with time and labor. Portraits, as well as written characters of men, should be decidedly marked, otherwise they will be insipid; and truth should be preferred before freedom of hand."

*Industry* and *economy* are homely virtues; but, like other homely handmaidens, they keep off the dust and rust of life. "Hogarth held that contest with fortune for bread, which is the usual lot of unfriended genius. Before the world felt his talents, and while he was storing his mind and his portfolio with nature and character, then was the season of fluctuating spirits, rising and falling hopes, churlish landladies, and importunate creditors. When he had conquered all these difficulties, he loved to dwell on these scenes of labor and privation, and fight over again the battle which ended so honorably to him as a man, and so gloriously to him as an artist. He was heard to say of himself, 'I remember the time when I have gone moping into the city with scarce a shilling, but as soon as I received ten guineas there for a plate, I have returned home, put on my sword, and sallied out again with all the confidence of a man who had thousands in his pockets.'

"With a head so clear, hands so clever, with youth and independent feelings on his side, he could not be destitute; and he never was."

Hogarth could not, for a long time, follow the bent of his original genius entirely. He had a mother and sisters in a measure dependent upon him, and success in his chosen path was uncertain; he made sure of his bread by engraving arms and crests. Silver bowls and tankards may yet be found in England, the engravings of which were done by Hogarth in his early days.

He embelished books with frontispieces and other illustrations. One of his biographers says, "No symptoms of genius dawned in those early plates;" and another adds, "But they are well worth examination, were it but to learn the lesson which genius reckons ungracious—that no distinction is to be obtained without long study and well-directed labor."

"I could do little more than maintain myself till I was near thirty," said the indefatigable artist; "but even then, *I was a punctual paymaster.*"

Hogarth, in the relations of son, brother, husband, and friend, was generous and indulgent; with regard to himself, he was abstemious, and frugal without parsimony; in his hospitalities, liberal and free-hearted.

The sculptor, Nollekens, and his wife, were "passing frugal people." By his persevering labor, the sculptor amassed a large fortune; and though he had occasional fits of generosity, it is to be lamented, that his economy degenerated into parsimony.

The king of Naples once said to the painter, Giotto, "Now, Giotto, if I were you, I would not labor so hard this hot weather." "Nor I, certainly," returned the painter, "if I were the king." Yet, that the labor, itself, was pleasure, no one can doubt; and, with the same genius, he would have felt impelled to labor, even had he been a king.

Among the virtues of the artist, should be named *kindness* and *generosity* to other artists, especially to such as are just struggling forward in the right path.

It was said of the noble Albrecht Durer, that "he knew not what it was to envy other artists; he rejoiced over everything that was good, and praised whatever there was to praise. If an ill-executed work was brought to him, he said, good-humoredly, 'Well, the master has done his best.' He was well versed in the Scriptures, and they furnished materials for his best representations. He never lent his talent to indecency; his art was as pure as his morals."

Charles V., of Spain, inquired Michel Angelo's opinion of Albrecht Durer. "Such is my esteem for him," replied he, "that, were I not Michel Angelo, I would prefer to be Durer even before Charles of Spain." Yet Michel Angelo is said to have been jealous of Raffaelle. On one occasion, when these two great painters were conversing, and admiring together a work of Andrew del Sarto, Michel Angelo, turning to Raffaelle, exclaimed, "yes, there is that little fellow in Florence, who, if he had been employed in great matters as thou art, would have made thee sweat again."

*Refinement* and *delicacy of sentiment,* may be named, among the "moralities" for an artist. No coarseness should pollute his canvas nor desecrate his marble. However tempted by lucre, he may not pander to vice, nor execute works for sensuality to gloat over. No; let him rather starve—die as a martyr to virtue—than thus to degrade noble Art to base purposes. Hundreds of years ago, was it said, or sung, by Sir Henry Walton:

"How happy is he born and taught,
  That serveth not another's will;
Whose armor is his honest thought,
  And simple truth his utmost skill:
*Whose passions not his master's are;*
  Whose soul is still prepared for death,
Untied unto the world by care
  Of public fame, or private breath."

## CHAPTER XVI.

### GENIUS WITHOUT VIRTUE.

Believe not that your inner eye
Can ever in just measure try
The worth of hours as they go by;

For every man's weak self, alas,
Makes him, to see them while they pass,
As through a dim or tinted glass.

Those surely are not fairly spent
That leave your spirit bowed and bent
In sad unrest and ill content.

So should we live, that every hour
May die as dies the natural flower,
A self-reviving thing of Power.—*Milnes.*

To secure the physical health of the living, men resort to the painful necessity of dissecting the dead; to secure moral health, similar dissections of human character are needful. Equally revolting, and equally painful are the two operations.

But "the evil that men do lives after them;" and therefore, in accordance with the law of self-preservation, that "evil" must be met in fair and open fight.

The aberrations of men of genius have done far more harm to the world than all the gross vices of the stupid and ignorant; they are excuses and palliatives for men of inferior minds; they are even imitated by dunces, who are capable of no other kind of emulation. Alas! for fallen human nature!

Gilbert Stuart went to London and was a pupil of Benjamin West. Col. Trumbull, the painter, saw him there in 1780, and thus describes his appearance: "He was dressed in an old black coat, with one half torn off the hip and pinned up, and looked more like a poor beggar than a painter." He was wretchedly poor while in London, and on one occasion, when he was sick, Trumbull called to see him; he found him in bed and apparently very ill. Sometime afterwards he asked Trumbull if he had any idea what was the matter with him. On being told that he had not, Stuart stated that it was hunger! He had eaten nothing in a week but sea-bread.

"He became a fashionable and leading artist in the great metropolis, where portrait painting has been carried to the highest perfection," says Dunlap. "From the commencement of his independent establishment as a portrait painter in London, success attended him, but *he was a stranger to prudence.* He lived in splendor, and was the gayest of the gay.* As he said of himself, he was a great beau. Pecu-

* Stuart never lost an opportunity for being merry. He was traveling, in England, in a stage-coach, with some gentlemen who were strangers to him, but all sociable and full of spirits. They stopped to dine; the conversation became animated and various. Stuart blazed away in his dramatic manner. His companions were very desirous to know who and what he was. To the round about question, to find out his calling or profession, Stuart answered with a grave face and serious tone, that he "sometimes dressed gentlemen's and

niary difficulties induced him to leave London for Dublin. There he met with disappointment. There is every reason to suppose that his total want of prudence, or extreme negligence and extravagance, had placed him in that situation which induces men

"To do such deeds as make the prosperous man
Lift up his hands, and wonder who could do them."

Stuart returned to his native country in 1793. "Stuart's appetites and passions were of the kind *said to be* uncontrollable; that is, they were indulged when present danger or inconvenience did not forbid. In New York, as elsewhere, the talents and acquirements of Stuart introduced him to the intimate society of all who were distinguished by office,

ladies' hair." "You are a hair-dresser, then?" "What!" said he, "do you take me for a barber?" "I beg your pardon, sir, but I inferred it from what you said. If I mistook you, may I take the liberty to ask what you are, then?" "Why, I sometimes *brush* a gentleman's coat, or hat, and sometimes adjust a cravat." "Oh, you are a valet, then, to some nobleman." "A valet! Indeed, sir, I am not; I am not a servant; to be sure I make coats and waistcoats for gentleman." "Oh, you are a tailor!" "Do I look like a tailor? I'll assure you I never handled any goose but a roasted one." "What are you, then?" exclaimed one. "I'll tell you," said Stuart. "Be assured all I have told you is literally true. I dress hair, brush hats and coats, waistcoats and breeches, and likewise *boots* and *shoes*—at your service." "Oho, a boot and shoemaker, after all!" "Guess again, gentlemen; I never handled boot or shoe, but for my own feet and legs; yet all I have told you is true." "We may as well give up querying."

After checking his laughter, he said to them very gravely: "Now, gentlemen, I will not play the fool with you any longer, but will tell you, upon my honor as a gentleman, my *bona fide* profession. I get rank, or attainment; and his observing mind and powerful memory rendered his conversation an inexhaustible fund of amusement and information to his sitters and his companions."

From New York Stuart went to Philadelphia, for the purpose of painting a portrait of Washington.

Stuart said he found more difficulty in expressing the character of Washington on the canvas than in any effort of the kind he had ever made. He could usually draw out the character of his sitters by his amusing colloquial efforts. But Stuart knew not what conversation to address to the dignified person before him, and lost self-possession. He finally succeeded, however, in producing one of the best portraits which was ever taken of Washington.

Judge Hopkinson has related an anecdote which explains, in part, the reason why Stuart suffered so much from

my bread *by making faces!*" He then screwed his countenance and twisted his visage in a manner that any comedian might have envied. When his companions, after loud peals of laughter, had composed themselves, each took credit to himself for having suspected all the while that the gentleman belonged to the theatre, and they all knew he must be a comedian by profession; when, to their utter surprise, he assured them he never was on the stage. They all now looked at each other with astonishment.

Before parting, Stuart said to his companions: "Gentlemen, you will find that all I have said of my various employments, is comprised in these few words: I am a portrait painter. If you will call at John Palmer's, York Buildings, London, there I shall be ready and willing to make you a coat or hat, dress your hair, *a la mode,* supply you, if in need, with a wig of any fashion or dimensions, accommodate you with boots or shoes, give you ruffles or cravats, and make faces for you."

poverty. "Cotemporary with our great portrait painter in the city of Penn, was a great wine-merchant, and it is well known that before his return to his native country, Stuart had contracted an unfortunate habit which rendered the dealers in wine very important personages in his estimation. It happened that the wine-merchant's taste for pictures was almost as strong as the painter's taste for Maderia, and he was willing to indulge Stuart's natural *palette* in exchange for the product of his artificial one. The wine-merchant had three portraits; value, per bill, three hundred dollars. When the painter and the wine-merchant balanced accounts, the dealer in paint and immortality, was debtor to the dealer in wine, per bill, two hundred dollars!"

"It should be borne in mind" said his friend, Dr. Waterhouse, "that Stuart had painted all the Presidents of the United States, the present one excepted, (1833,) and most of the distinguished characters of the Revolution, and that Sir Joshua Reynolds himself sat to him, and that take him altogether he was one of the most extraordinary men our country has produced." "With the most brilliant talents, and through life, the admiration of every one who approached him, or saw his works."

Gilbert Stuart died poor. How many without a hundreth part of his talents have passed through life by their own efforts, not only without embarrassment from poverty, but in affluence, merely by following the dictates of prudence and conscience. With reference to more than his want of affluence, it may be said, as was said of another professor of the fine arts, "poorly, poor man, he lived, poorly, poor man, he died."

It is sad, indeed, thus to record the aberrations of men of genius, but warning is as needful to the young as encouragement. There are peculiar temptations lying all along in the path of the artist, and such an example, as that of Stuart, utters aloud—Beware! Beware!

# CHAPTER XVII.

## THE MANHOOD OF THE ARTIST.

### DOMESTIC LIFE.

"The artist has a double existence, one in imagination and in his works, the other as a man in his home; and each pervades, completes, and supports the other, and neither is long, without the other, good and available."—*Artist's Married Life.*

No man on earth more imperatively needs a *home*, a quiet, peaceful home, than the artist. His absorbing pursuits, in a measure, unfit him for the petty cares of this every day "bank-note world." Who shall relieve him from the burden, or bear it with him?

"A being breathing thoughtful breath,
A traveler betwixt life and death;
The reason firm, the temperate will,
Endurance, foresight, strength and skill;
A perfect woman nobly planned,
*To warn, to comfort and command.*"

The opinion has come to be too general, that an artist must forego the comforts of domestic life. "Are you married yet?" enquired a friend of an artist, who had not seen him for several years. "Certainly not," was the reply; "painting is my wife."

Men of superior genius, whose lives were a protracted martyrdom, may have done more for posterity than the sculptor

Flaxman; but there are few happier lives than his on record. The manhood of Flaxman was perfectly consistent with his grave and quiet childhood, his industrious and moral boyhood.

"In the year 1782 he quitted the paternal roof, hired a small house and studio in Wardaur street, collected a stock of choice materials, set his sketches in good order, and took unto himself a wife, Ann Denman, *one whom he had long loved*, and who deserved his affection. She was amiable and accomplished, had a taste for art and literature, was skillful in French and Italian, and, like her husband, had acquired some knowledge of Greek. But what was better than all, she was an enthusiastic admirer of his genius—she cheered and encouraged him in his moments of despondency—regulated modestly and prudently his domestic economy—arranged his drawings—managed now and then his correspondence—and acted in all particulars as though the church, in performing their marriage, had accomplished a miracle; and blended them really into one flesh and one blood.

The sculptor, happy in the company of one who had taste and enthusiasm, soon renewed with double zeal the studies which courtship and matrimony had interrupted. He had never doubted that in the company of the wife whom he loved he should be able to work with an intense spirit; but of another opinion was that confirmed old bachelor, Sir Joshua Reynolds.

"So Flaxman," said Sir Joshua, one day, as he chanced

to meet him, "I am told you are married; if so, sir, I tell you, you are ruined for an artist!"

Flaxman went home, sat down beside his wife, took her hand and said, with a smile, "I am ruined for an artist."

"John," said she, "how has this happened, and who has done it?"

"It happened," said he, "in the church, and Ann Denman has done it; I met Sir Joshua Reynolds just now, and he said marriage had ruined me in my profession."

But was it so? No, indeed. Flaxman and his good little wife were not to be frightened by the sneer of the testy old bachelor; they went on quietly in their own way, determined to disprove his assertion. They asked no advice of others; they shared their domestic concerns with none of their neighbors, and lived apparently unconscious of the stir and strife of a great city.

"Ann," said the sculptor, "I have long thought that I could not rise to distinction in art without studying in Italy, but these words of Reynolds' have determined me. I shall go to Rome, as soon as my affairs are fit to be left; and to show him that wedlock is for a man's good, rather than for his harm, you shall accompany me."

In this resolution Mrs. Flaxman fully concurred. They resolved to consult no one, and in order to accomplish the undertaking without assistance, they determined to practice strict economy. It was five years after the disheartening speech of Sir Joshua before they were able to realize their pet plan.

One who knew Flaxman well has given a discription of his household as follows: "I remember his humble little house in Wardaur street. All was neat, nay, elegant; the figures from which he studied were the finest antiques, the nature which he copied was the fairest that could be had, and all in his studio was propriety and order. But what struck me most, was the air of devout quiet which reigned everywhere; the models which he made, and the designs which he drew, were not more serene than he was himself, and his wife had that meek composure of manner which he so much loved in art.

Yet, better than all was the devout feeling of this singular man; there was no ostentatious display of piety; nay, he was in some sort a lover of mirth and sociality, but he was a reader of the Scriptures,* and a worshiper of sincerity, and if ever purity visited the earth she resided with John Flaxman."

It is also recorded of him that he visited suffering widows and orphans, and relieved them frequently by small donations, and gave it to them privately that he might not be seen by men.

In 1787 Flaxman and his wife went to Rome, where he studied with intense delight the remains of ancient art.

* "I have but one book, sir," said the poet Collins, "but that is the best."

"Into these works he looked with the eye of a sculptor and of a Christian." He resolved that if possible all his future works in sculpture should embody passages of Holy Writ, and exhibit the divine dispensation of our blessed Saviour.

But in Rome, as eleswhere, Flaxman was obliged to labor for his support, and was therefore obliged to follow in part the taste of the persons for whom he executed works of art. He illustrated Homer, Æschylus and Dante.

"Long ere this time of life he had shown, in numerous instances, that he regarded gold only as a thing to barter for food and raiment, and which enabled him to realize, in benevolent deeds, the generous wishes of his heart. As a fountain whence splendor, honor and respect might flow, he never considered it; and in a plain dress, and from a frugal table, he appeared among the rich and the titled, neither seeking their notice nor shunning it. In all these sentiments his wife shared.

Those who desire to see Flaxman aright during his seven years' study in Italy, must not forget to admit into the picture the modest matron who was ever at his side, aiding him by her knowledge and directing him by her taste. They loved each other truly—they read the same books—thought the same thoughts—prized the same friends—were at peace with each other, and had no wish to be separated. Their residence was in the Via Felice; and all who wished to be distinguished for taste or genius were visitors of the sculptor's humble abode.

Enjoying thus the sweetest domestic happiness, he had no disturbing forces to operate against his progress in his chosen profession. He felt deeply his indebtedness to his wife, and testified it in a touching and peculiar manner.

"He caused a little quarto book to be made, containing some score or two of leaves, and with pen and pencil proceeded to embellish it. On the first page is drawn a dove, with an olive branch in her mouth; an angel is on the right, and an angel on the left, and between is written, '*To Ann Flaxman;*' below, two hands are clasped as at the altar, two cherubs bear a garland, and the following inscription to his wife introduces the subject:

"The anniversary of your birthday calls on me to be grateful for fourteen happy years passed in your society. Accept the tribute of these sketches, which, under the allegory of a knight-errant's adventures, indicate the trials of virtue and the conquest of vice, preparatory to a happier state of existence. After the hero is called to the spiritual world, and blessed with a celestial union, he is armed with power for the exercise of his ministry, and for fulfilling the dispensations of Providence; he becomes the associate of Faith, Hope, and Charity, and as Universal Benevolence, is employed in acts of mercy.—John Flaxman, October 2d, 1796."

The designs which tell this noble story amount to forty. There is much poetic dignity in the conception of this *poem*, (for such I must call it,) and as much in the handling; nor do I know of anything in the whole compass of our works of genius with which it can be more aptly compared than Spencer's Fairy Queen.

It was the object of Flaxman to exhibit his "Knight of the Burning Cross," fulfilling all the duties which our Saviour enjoined. This "grand moral poem" was executed in pencil sketches of great beauty, and must have been a most acceptable offering to that excellent wife.

"Flaxman was gay, cheerful and companionable; he was not one of those who take their mirth abroad, and reserve moroseness for home. He would often cheer the winter evening by composing light and amusing things for the entertainment of his family, or his friends; ingenious little stories in prose or verse, illustrated with sketches, serious and burlesque. Much of the peculiar talent of the man found its way into those unstudied trifles; in his hand the merriest legend failed not to put on a moral aim and a classic grace.

"For thirty-eight years Flaxman enjoyed uninterrupted domestic happiness. His wife continued the same cheerful, intelligent companion that she had been in their early wedded life. Her husband's respect and affection were such as any woman would consider beyond all price. She had aided him in his profession, sympathized in his trials, kept up the steady glow of his enthusiasm, and been the light and joy of his home. When any criticisms, with regard to English composition, took place at his table or fireside, he would say, with a smile, 'Ask Mrs. Flaxman, she is my dictionary.'

"She maintained the simplicity and dignity of her husband, and refused all presents unless some reciprocal interchange were made. Could it be otherwise, than that the gentle, affectionate Flaxman should love such a woman tenderly? The hour of their earthly separation came in the year 1820.

"From the time of this bereavement, a lethargy came over the spirit of the sculptor; she, who had shared in all his joys and sorrows, was gone, and nothing could comfort him. Their separation was of short duration. In less than six years he followed to the world of spirits."

The inscription on his tomb is as follows:

"John Flaxman, R. A. P. S., whose mortal life was a constant preparation for a blessed immortality; his angelic spirit returned to the Divine Giver on the 7th of December, 1826, in the seventy-second year of his age."

Such a life needs no comment.

## CHAPTER XVIII.

### REASONS FOR BECOMING AN ARTIST.

"The busy world shoves angrily aside,
The man who stands with arms akimbo,
Until occasion tells him what to do."—*Lowell.*

"We judge ourselves by what we are capable of doing; others judge us by what we have done."

The first and chief reason for any one's being an artist, is, because such was evidently the design of Providence. Well might the monarch say he could make noblemen, but God alone could make such artists as Michel Angelo.* To fulfill His own all-wise purposes, He has bestowed various gifts upon men, and in various degrees.

There is no difficulty in finding out what these gifts are, in each individual case, if early development be carefully watched. Did any one doubt that Salvator Rosa† might become a painter, after they had seen what he could produce with the end of a burnt stick, the only pencil he could command? Perhaps the monks, who soundly whipped the boy for drawing on the walls of their chapel, thought the propensity might be whipped out of him, or, at least, that he might

* Henry VIII. said, of seven peasants he could make seven noblemen, but he could not make one Hans Holbein.

† Born near Naples, 1615.

be whipped into the church, for which his parents had designed him. He was greatly indebted, however, to the well-meaning monks, for they sent him to school, where he acquired a good classical education; but nothing could divert him from following the bent of his genius.

A father may say, as he lays his hand upon the clustering curls of his first-born boy—"This son I will make a lawyer; this next fair-haired laddie, I will make a clergyman; and as for the brave boy, still in his nurse's arms, he shall be an artist."

Allons! *make* the first a lawyer; educate him from childhood for that profession, but should he have been designed for an artist, his books, perchance, will display ornamented margins of his own drawing, and the walls of his bed-room give the same proofs of his inventive faculty, as did those of Salvator Rosa. Try again with the next. He will not be a lawyer, but his vocation you had hit upon in the first place, he will be a clergyman. As for the youngster—"Why may not that be the scull of a lawyer?" In due time he is crammed with Latin and Greek, and sent to college, stoutly rebelling all the while against the procedure; he is not building "castles in the air," but the time that he should have devoted to the classics is employed upon designs for real, substantial buildings—the boy will be an architect. This original capacity, or aptitude, for certain pursuits, is now very generally acknowledged; yet it is almost invariably overlooked when the *choice* of a *pro-*

*fession* or *trade* is under consideration. When pride, or interest comes in the way, then, circumstances make the man; they say—he may as well use the intellect for one purpose as for another.

They do not deny that there is gradation—from an idiot to a Newton—but they for the nonce deny, that Newton had any more capacity from nature, for mathematics, than he had for sculpture; only that circumstances determined him into that particular course of mental action. The original sameness of the human capacity! The original material of diamond and charcoal! The same—the very same—therefore they are precisely alike, and you may set the charcoal in gold and surround it with pearls, and use diamonds to raise the steam for one of Collins' ocean monsters.

Nothing can be more absurd, than this notion of original sameness. How many lives, in consequence of it, have been worse than wasted. How many have drudged in dull discontent, on the tread-mill to which they had been consigned by misjudging friends.

On the other hand, how many have ambitiously aspired to what was beyond their reach!

Because a boy dislikes school, it is no proof that he would like mechanical labor. He may be only lazy. But if the same boy finds, from day to day, the acquisition of knowledge from books an exceedingly irksome task, and leaves the school-room with joy, to go to a neighboring brook, where he is building a bridge; if he there labors incessantly and effectively till he has built a good bridge—and demonstrates that he has mechanical talent—then he had better build bridges for the rest of his life, than study Greek and Latin, preparatory to making a very poor scholar.

The boy may be clever enough about everything else but the very thing, for which his anxious parents have designed him.

Then, again, he may rebel against nature, and endeavor to thwart her designs. He may say, I will not be an artist, for artists are always poor as fishes: I must be rich—I will be a merchant. No, no, my boy; if you possess true genius, you will not long be of that opinion. You will spurn such a low thought—you will so delight in following out the promptings of genius, that paltry pelf will only for a brief space come between you and those visions of beauty, which will soon engross all thought and effort. By some wonderful power of adaptation, or some inscrutable law, most men find, like water, their level. Some unfortunates, indeed, continue buried under mountains of difficulty all their lives; but others burst all opposing obstacles, and like geysers, astonish mankind.

But training—training; if the boy will submit to it, he can be trained and gently led the way we wish.

Can you train a woodbine to twine around a column from west to east? will it not pertinaciously adhere to the bent which nature has given it, and *insist* upon going from east to west? Could Walter Scott have been Dr. Johnson? or

Dr. Franklin, Milton? Could Wordsworth have been Napoleon? or Thorwaldsen, Wellington?

An acorn and a hazelnut bear some resemblance to each other—plant them in the same soil, bestow upon them the same culture—the acorn will produce the noble oak tree, the hazelnut only a stunted bush.

You cannot make a dwarf a giant, by stretching him all his life on a Procrustean bed; neither can you entirely dwarf a giant, by reversing the process; though you may rob him, in a degree, of his fair proportions. There is mental as well as physical stature—there is a mould in which the mind is cast, and from which it takes its form and pressure, as truly as there is a mould for the hazelnut and the acorn.

Did the father of Shakspeare, the ignorant woolcomber, educate Shakspeare for a dramatist? Were there any *circumstances* in his early life, that predisposed the boy to philosophy and poetry? Who taught Giotto painting? Not Cimabue, his reputed master, though Giotto has been said to be the greatest work that ever came out of that master's studio. Who taught Pascal geometry? Not his father, who shut up all mathematical books from his sight, so that the boy was obliged to draw diagrams upon the floor and walls of his room, and invent problems for himself. Who gave Michel Angelo, Raffaelle, and Leonardo da Vinci the *impulse* which impelled each and all of them to be architects, painters and sculptors? Neither popes nor cardinals, neither monarchs nor merchant princes, though they wondered at their inborn greatness, and delighted to honor them, in life and in death.* The eye of one man sees no farther than his hand can reach; another takes in the whole creation at a glance, and lights it up with a living glow. One man sees in the resplendent rivers, only grand water-powers; and another, in the sublimest of cataracts, a "nice place to sponge cloth;" while to the lover of beauty and sublimity, they reveal a "present Deity," and call forth exultant admiration.

We may go still farther. One painter is a good colorist, he has an eye for color. Sir Joshua Reynolds, though he professed to admire, almost to idolatry, the genius of Michel Angelo, could never imitate him in form and composition—his forte was color, and portrait painting. West was skillful in composition, but detestable as a colorist. Titian's coloring was inimitable, but, in other respects, he was inferior to Rembrandt. Another painter can represent nature, like Claude Lorraine, in landscape, while he cannot portray the "human face divine." Hogarth learned that his forte lay, in that world of truth and nature, where the ludicrous and pathetic are so mysteriously blended, and gave up the painting of grand historic subjects to men of different natural abilities.

There are some painters who have little invention, but large imitative faculties. These are the portrait painters.

* Leonardo da Vinci died, reclining on the bosom of Francis I. of France.

Imitation was eminently the leading characteristic of the late Sir Thomas Lawrence. Now, imitation may be said to be far inferior to the inventive faculty; so far as to be undeserving of the name of genius, which is in its very nature creative. Genius is both imitative and creative. When a painter executes works equal to those of Lawrence, we cannot safely deny that he possesses *genius* for portrait painting. From the child and savage, up to the man of the strongest intellectual power and most refined culture, there is pleasure felt in viewing a successful imitation—the *look of life* which cheats the eye.

Sir Thomas Lawrence added to this charm that of a delicate touch and fine coloring. Moreover, the attitudes, the accessories, the very drapery of his portraits aided in giving the predominant character of the individual represented. "His lords are prodigiously lordly," says an English critic; "his senators are the very men in their best looks, whom we see in the two Houses; shrewd, sagacious, and reflecting — conscious of power and privilege: and never doubting the result of the next election. Is it to be wondered at that this artist was eminently popular? There is much in his pictures that is delightful, and nothing that can displease. He makes no demand upon our imaginations with which they are unable to comply. With him we are in a pleasant valley, beside a quiet stream, and the Naiades and Dryades are all the most polished ladies and gentlemen. He does not place us on the brink of some grand, but tremendous precipice, and make our weak brains whirl with giddiness as we look down. His lakes are always in sunshine, and gently curled with a spring breeze; and his rivers at no season of the year are flooded to torrents. But there are feelings in the human heart, which a painter may awaken, far nobler and more stirring than those produced by such objects."

As an instance of a far higher order of genius, Martin is contrasted with Lawrence by the same critic. "No painter," says this enthusiastic admirer of Martin, "has ever like him represented the immensity of space—none like him made architecture so sublime, merely through its vastness; no painter, like him, has spread forth the boundless valley, or piled mountain upon mountain to the sky—like him has none made light pour down in dazzling floods from heaven; and none, like him, has painted the 'darkness visible of the infernal deeps.'"

Martin, fortunately, like Hogarth, struck into his own peculiar path, and has kept it faithfully. That path lies by the vast, the magnificent, the terrific, the supernatural. Who but Martin could have painted *his* FEAST OF BELSHAZZAR?

"A wicked and arrogant king sits with his thousand lords, his wives and his concubines, at the feast, and impiously profanes the vessels which had been consecrated to the worship of the One God: but the gods of gold and of silver, of brass, of iron, of wood and of stone, they praise and worship. The measure of his guilt is full, and the punishment must follow. But, in the face of all has the crime been perpetrated, and before the eyes of all must his doom be announced. In the height of their sacrilegious banquet, a hand, an armless hand, writes upon the wall the irrevocable words, and having written them disappears. Then is the king's countenance changed and his thoughts trouble him, so that the joints of his loins are unloosed, and his knees smite one against another. The astrologers and the soothsayers strive in vain to read the unknown characters; but the prophet of God appears and interprets them to the king. This is the subject of the picture—a theme grand, awful and difficult. It is not a subject for a *fine colorist* merely, or an *expert draughtsman*, but for a *poet* who can embody his conceptions in form and color."

The painter makes the daring attempt to represent "a scene in which the Deity himself, not all invisibly working, is an immediate agent."

He produces an overwhelming awe arising from the mysterious and awful hand writing upon the wall. That sublime hand writing—the MENE, MENE, TEKEL—glares with supernatural light upon an entablature of the magnificent palace of the king. The "hand" has left it there, to affright the monarch and his courtiers, to confound the Chaldeans and astrologers, and to be read alone by the prophet of God.

The fearful letters cast their vivid glare upon the ghastly faces of the bewildered crowd, and the once brilliant lamps of the festal hall, "pale their ineffectual fires."

The vast and massive architecture imparts a solemn grandeur to the scene, while its calm immobility contrasts strikingly with the panic and phrensy of the multitude. "A tremendous tower, buried in clouds, and darkly visible under the flaring of the distant lightning, looks grimly over the roofless palace-hall, as if its impious builders had indeed made its top reach unto the heaven. Every thing in this wonderful picture combines to excite and sustain that emotion of sublime and supernatural awe, which is the ruling sentiment, the very soul of the subject." It was Martin's special mission to paint that picture and others of a similar character.

## CHAPTER XIX.

### INCENTIVES AND DISCOURAGEMENTS.

"The way to be an excellent painter is to be an excellent man. And these united make a character that would shine in a better world than this."—*Richardson.*

It has been said that our country yet offers few encouragements to the artist. This might have been said with truth twenty or thirty years ago, but now there are abounding facts to disprove the assertion. Orders come to our best artists faster than they can execute them.

The Americans have been called "a *mechanical* people;" time and opportunity granted, and they will become eminently *artistical.* They are not a phlegmatic people, insensible to the charms of Nature and the beauties of Art. They are hardy and mercurial, imitative and ingenious. The mixture of all nations here, and the powerful influence of climate, have produced a modification of the Anglo-Saxon character, differing widely from the home-born and home-bred English. Its elements, of course, are the same, but the sombre clay has been kneaded up with a goodly quantity of *quicksilver.* The English have never been remarkable for elegance and taste; they have never produced the finest models in art, excepting in architecture, and that was of lang syne; but they can boast of being very respectable artists.

This they acknowledge, or did thirty years ago. Perhaps they may say, "we have changed all these things now." Thirty years ago one of their ablest writers said: "An Englishman does not ordinarily pretend to combine his own gravity, plainness and reserve, with the levity, loquacity, grimace, and artificial politeness, *as it is called,* of the Frenchman. Why, then, will he insist upon engrafting the fine upon the domestic arts, as an indispensable consummation of the national character? We may, indeed, cultivate them as an experiment in natural history, and produce specimens of them, and exhibit them as rarities in their kind, as we do hot-house plants and shrubs; but they are not of native growth or origin. They do not sit as graceful ornaments, but as excrescences on the English character; they are like 'flowers in our caps, dying ere they sicken;' they are exotics and aliens to the soil. We do not import foreigners to dig our canals, or construct our machines, or solve difficult problems in political economy, or write Scotch novels for us; but we import our dancing masters, our opera singers, our valets and our cooks, as *till lately* we did our painters and sculptors.

"The progress of the fine arts has been slow and wavering, and unpromising in our country, and their encouragement has been cold and backward in proportion."

Our own country, these United States, is now rich enough to patronize artists, and the people are sufficiently cultivated, by foreign travel and domestic education, to appreciate genius. They are improving in taste. They have, moreover, patriotism enough to be willing to encourage native talent. But setting aside patriotism, who does not prefer one of Cole's landscapes of American scenery, to a host of the tame productions of modern Italian artists? Who does not infinitely prefer the "Greek Slave" to all the statues modern France has produced?

The Americans are accused of boastfulness. They have been so often basely maligned and so severely ridiculed, that they have been compelled to defend themselves, and in so doing have, perhaps, made too great a flourish of trumpets—but we may modestly boast of our artists, without gainsaying.

West was an American—Copley became a good artist before he went abroad. Leslie commenced painting in this country. Trumbull, Stuart, Vanderlyn, Cole, Inman, were native artists. Allston, and a host of living painters, whom it would be a pleasure to name, have ably vindicated our claim to genius in that branch of the fine arts. Our sculptors, too, have wide-world fame. Our architects—"look around"—they do not "hide their light under a bushel."

There is encouragement of another kind to the artist in this country, which does not exist in England. "Art," said Allan Cunningham, "has not yet become with us a *fashionable profession for the gentlemen and scholar!* Sir Thomas Lawrence was the son of an inn-keeper. Jackson, of a tailor. Gainsborough, the son of a clothier, etc., etc." What then? They became distinguished men, and the first, especially, had every claim to the title of gentleman. Artists, from time immemorial, have shone like fixed stars by their own light, while "honors possessed by heritage, are like stars seen in the ocean, which were never there but for the originals in heaven." Painting, sculpture and architecture are among the *liberal* arts, and the son of the most distinguished statesman in America does not "lose caste" by becoming a painter. Far from it; our painters have been "scholars and gentlemen." Though we are not bound by the fetters of "*caste*" yet there is here an "aristocracy"—the aristocracy of talent—the highest round on the ladder of aristocracy—*excepting*, that of goodness.

"The first nobleman in the land,"* says an English writer, "may practice painting, as *an amusement*, may devote to it much of his time and may attain a proficiency equal to that of a professional artist, without it being considered derogatory to his rank; but if the tenth son of the lowest baron were to follow painting as a profession, there would be many well-meaning, ridiculous persons who would hold up their hands in surprise and horror at such a step. Painting is treated as a mechanical art, and the man of rank would be considered to *lose caste* by following it. Now, without summoning to our aid that undeniable principle, that there is no real disgrace in any honest calling, or taking higher and sounder ground of argument than the customs and

* Even in the royal family of Great Britain, as well as among the nobility, there have been *amateur* sculptors.

prejudices of society, we must say, that there seems to be something very unreasonable in this exclusion of the art of painting from such professions as a gentleman is at liberty to follow. Why should the announcement from a nobleman, that one of his younger sons discovers a strong bent for painting, and will, therefore, become a painter by profession, be answered, as it would, by a stare and a shrug, and remain a theme of wonder and reproach? Society admits that a peer may, without shame, sell the productions of his pen, why might he not dispose of the productions of his pencil? If the Honorable Mr. Such-a-one, a barrister, may take guinea fees without contamination, why may he not equally, without disgrace, paint a picture, send it to an exhibition, and sell it for a hundred pounds?"

For no reason in the world that ought to have the least weight with a rational being untrammeled by narrow conventionalisms. These strange notions are the more remarkable in England, where artists, once acknowledged to possess genius, find easy access into the highest social "*caste.*"

Sir Joshua Reynolds, West and Lawrence, were the companions even of royalty, and mingled with some of the most aristocratic society in England; the same may be said of some eminent artists of the present day.

Happily, there are no such artificial restrictions in our country at the very outset. There is nothing humiliating in the very apprenticeship of art. A young man may choose to be an architect, a painter, or a sculptor, without encountering sneers and scoffs, stares and shrugs, excepting from the aristocracy of wealth, who will tell him, perhaps, that it is not a rapid way to make money, and that he had better go into the "grocery business."

Another inducement to follow art, as a profession, is the pleasure that the pursuit affords. The preparatory studies are delightful. The objects to which the young artist's attention must be directed are the most beautiful and most interesting in the whole field of nature, literature and art.

It is a refined, intellectual pursuit. Every branch of art requires the exercise of ideality. The boldest imagination and the most delicate sensibility are requisites for the higher efforts of art.

In portrait painting, the greatest excellence is unattainable unless the artist has familiarity with the graces of deportment, and the elegance of manner and expression which only habits of society can give. He will *put his own life* even into his portraits. He will, therefore, seek and enjoy the society of *the refined* and *the intellectual,* though he may be frequently called to perpetuate the features of persons who have no claim to these two attributes.

Ever since Giotto was the friend of Dante, Petrarch, and Boccaccio, artists have been *the companions and friends of literary men,* and that companionship, beside giving stimulus to the imagination, and strength to the intellect, has been a never-failing fountain of pleasure. The enthusiasm of a genuine artist will surround his employment with a halo of happiness. In his studio the wise, the good, the beautiful, are his silent teachers. Secluded from the stir and bustle of life, he has the quiet enjoyment denied to men who mingle in political strife, who contend on the legal arena, or fight the real battles of their country on sea and land. His

"Mind to him a kingdom is,"

from which he looks out, as from a high watch-tower, or noble fortress, on the passions, the cabals, the meannesses, and follies of mankind. He may, if he choose, shut himself up in "measureless content," execute his noble works, and appeal from envious detractions, or "unjust tribunals," to posterity.

The landscape painter flies from the blank walls of the crowded city, to copy nature in her romantic retreats. There, conversing with her rudest or her most graceful forms, "lost in lonely musing—eyeing the clouds that roll over his head, or listening to the water-fall, or seeing the fresh breeze waving the mountain pines, or leaning against the side of an impending rock," he hears not the jarring and creaking wheels of artificial life.

"He holds communion with nature," and when he returns to his studio his memory is filled with "visible forms" of beauty, which with ready skill he will transfer to the canvas.

The sculptor, alone at night in his studio, with the suspended lamp shedding its rays upon the marble before him, need not envy the flutterers of fashion in the crowded assembly. He has a higher joy, as one by one he brings out the features which have long haunted his imagination, and gives to the work of his hands, expression, character, beauty, all but Promethean fire. The architect, as the noble building shapes itself in his mind, and the many parts assume form and proportion, has similar enjoyment. The artist is not like the mere money-getter, using means (not always agreeable ones,) to accomplish a certain end; to him there is positive enjoyment in the means; he may truly say, *Labor ipse voluptas:*—work, itself, is pleasure. The enthusiasm of Michel Angelo was so great, that he seemed to have a kind of fury against the marble which concealed from him his statue.*

And after a fine work is completed, how great must be the pleasure of the artist? But, alas! like every thing human, art has trials for its votaries, many and various.

* In a book, written in the sixteenth century, by Blaire de Vegencie, we find the following:—

"Je puis dire d'avoir vu Michel Ange, âgé de plus de soixante ans, et avec un corps maigre qu'étoit bien loin d'annoncer la force, faire voler en un quart d'heure plus d'éclats d'un marbre très dur, que n'auroient pu faire en une heure trois jeunes sculpteurs des plus forts: chose presqu'incroyable à qui ne l'a pas vu. Il y allait avec tant d'impetuosité et tant de furie, que je craignois à tout moment de voir le bloc entier tomber en pièces. Chaque coup faisoit voler à terre des éclats de trois ou quatre doigts d'épaisseur, et il appliquoit son ciseau si près de l'extrême contour, que si l'éclat eût avancé d'une ligne tout étoit perdu. Brulé par l'image du beau qui lui apparaissoit, et qu'il craignoit de perdre, ce grand homme avoit une espèce de fureur contre le marbre qui lui cachoit sa statue."

First and foremost, the artist fears *poverty*. Let him look the demon in the face, and he will find that he is not so dark as he has been painted.

When poets ate their dry crust in a garret and did not aspire beyond Grub Street, other artists might expect to starve entirely. And they did so, even in Italy, the boasted home of art.

Pietro Perugino, the master of Raffaelle, "having quitted his extreme destitution in Perugio, and betaken himself to Florence, sought, by means of excellence, to arrive at a certain station. He continued for many months, for want of a better bed, to sleep wretchedly in a chest; turned night into day, and applied himself incessantly to study his profession. The terrors of poverty being ever before his eyes, he did things to obtain money, which he would not even have looked at, if he had had the means of maintaining himself." "*How great a benefit to men of genius, poverty is?*" continues Vascari, "and how powerful a cause of becoming perfect and excellent in any art whatever? It is possible that riches would have closed against Perugino the path of becoming excellent, as completely as poverty opened it to him, and want spurred him on. In seeking to raise himself as an artist, he regarded not cold or hunger, discomfort or inconveniences, labor or shame; saying always, as it were for a proverb, that after the bad, the good weather must at last come, and that when the weather is good the people make themselves houses, that they may be able to remain under shelter in time of need.'"

Salvator Rosa had the same powerful incentive to exertion as Perugino. Lady Morgan, in her fanciful Life of Salvator, describes the youthful artist after he had fled from the restraints of an uncongenial home, as follows: "Sometimes he was discovered by the Padre cercatore of the convent of Renella, among the rocks and caverns of Baiæ, the ruined temples of gods and the haunts of sybils. Sometimes he was found sleeping among the wastes of the Solfatara, beneath the scorched branches of a blasted tree, his head pillowed by lava (a worse bed than Perugino's chest,) and his dream, most probably, the vision of an infant poet's slumbers. For even there he was

> 'The youngest he
> That sat in shadow of Apollo's tree,
> Seeing nature with a poet's eye, and
> Sketching nature with a poet's hand.'"

But to hawk those "sketches" about the streets of Naples, and part with what was so dear and rich to him, for a few pieces of copper—there was no poetry in that! Thankfully be it acknowledged, that no artist in our country need be hungry and houseless:—

> "There is bread and work enough for all."

No sooner are his works—if they bear indubitable marks of genius—no sooner are they exhibited to the public—if it be only in a shop-window—than patronage of the most substantial kind follows—the patronage of the people, more sure and more lasting than that of monarchs. There is an almost universal fondness for decoration among the people, and few houses are so poor, that they have not some pictorial ornaments; even the cell of the prisoner and the *parlor* of the insane pauper, are thus ornamented. True, these pictures may be merely coarse prints, but frequently they are copies from the best masters. The number of copies of the "Madonna della Seggiola" of Raffaelle, of all kinds now in existence, would be a curious and incredible fact. The number that have been taken since the original was completed would be astonishing. The annals of genius in our country are not darkened by the mournful accounts of men starving to death like Chatterton, or, dying in jail in "utter wretchedness and penury," like Morland.

Yet our artists have sufficient spur to exertion—they usually hold their life on the tenure, "work or die."

Another hindrance to artists, arises from *morbid sensibility*. Too frequently they are wayward, impatient of restraint, jealous and irritable. "Those who are at war with others, are not at peace with themselves."

"Salvator Rosa was rejected by the Academy of Saint Luke, and in consequence of his hostility to reigning authorities, and his unlicensed freedom of speech, excluded from the great works and public buildings in Rome; and though he scorned and ridiculed those by whose influence this was effected, yet neither the smiles of friends and fortune, nor the flatteries of fame, which in his lifetime had spread his name over Europe, and might be confidently expected to extend it to a future age, could console him for the loss which he affected to despise, and would make no sacrifices to obtain. He was, indeed, hard to please. He denounced his rivals and maligners with bitterness; and with difficulty tolerated the enthusiasm of his disciples, or the services of his patrons. He was at all times full of indignation with or without cause. He was easily exasperated, and not willing soon to be appeased, or to subside into repose and good humor again. He slighted what he did best, and seemed anxious to go out of himself." It must be confessed, that irritability rather than morbid sensibility was the infirmity of Salvator Rosa's character; yet the former might have arisen from the latter.

"The savage landscapes of Salvator Rosa are such as might have been expected from the violence and restlessness of his disposition; it is not surprising that he did not succeed in historic painting. The painter of humanity should be kindly and loving, discriminating and just.

"Salvator Rosa, is, beyond all question, the most *romantic* of landscape painters, because the very violence and intractableness of his temper threw him, with instinctive force, upon those objects in nature, which would be most likely to soothe and disarm it; while in history he is little less than a caricaturist, because the same acrimony and impatience have made him fasten on those subjects and aspects of the human mind, which would most irritate and increase it; and he has, in this department, produced chiefly distortion and deformity, sullenness and rage, extravagance, squalidness, and poverty of appearance."

"Salvator, a man originally endowed with higher powers than Claude Lorraine," says Ruskin, "*was altogether unfaithful to his mission,* and has left us, I believe, no gift. Everything that he did, is evidently for the sake of exhibiting his own dexterity; there is no *love* of any kind for anything; his choice of landscape features is distinguished by no delight in the sublime, but by mere animal restlessness and ferocity, guided by an imaginative power, of which he could not altogether deprive himself."

Would any one for a moment believe, that Raffaelle possessed a similar character, judging from his historical paintings? Could that loving mother, the Madonna della Seggiola, have been portrayed by a man of savage rudeness and ferocious irritability? No; we see the artist in his works as we do the poet. We do not doubt the verisimilitude of the following portrait of Raffaelle: "He had a regular, agreeable, and delicate face, the features well-proportioned, the hair brown, the eyes the same color, full of sweetness and modesty; the tone of the face bordering upon the olive; the expression that of grace and sensibility. The rest of his conformation seems to have been completely in harmony with his physiognomy. His manners were full of charm; his exterior was prepossessing; his style of dress elegant, announcing an acquaintance with the usages of the world, and what is called the *ton* of the court people. His moral qualities, those of the heart and mind, corresponded to the charm and grace of his person. One is touched with the gratitude he never ceased to exhibit to his old master, Perugino, and, above all, with the respect he paid to his works, and the care he had for his reputation. He associated Perugino's portrait with his own in many compositions, as if to make him share the honor of a talent, which owed to him its first direction. It does not appear that the feeling of envy ever had possession of his heart. Although it is impossible, for the artist not to compare himself with those who surround him, and though Raffaelle did not omit to institute such comparisons, yet his conduct and his works show only noble emulation. The envious man studies only how to lower his rivals, in order to rise on their ruins—to despoil them only to enrich himself at their expense. The genuine, the generous rival, takes nothing from those whom he competes with; he does not even borrow from them; if he owes them anything, it is only the necessity of the effort he is to make, in order to combat them; and even when he triumphs over them, he refers to them the glory of his success. Just towards all, Raffaelle knew how to render homage to his most dangerous rivals; and he was heard to thank God that he was born in the time of Michel Angelo.* En-

* "Michel Angelo, the stoic Michel Angelo, living alone, and working alone, formed, by his sombre humor, his unsocial character, in

dowed with a rare obligingness, even towards comparative strangers, he was never known to refuse his services to any. Ever ready to lay aside his own work for that of other people, he gave advice, and even designs, to those who claimed his aid. His cotemporaries have lauded his extreme benevolence towards all, his charity towards the unfortunate."

Raffaelle died at the early age of thirty-seven. His loss caused universal grief and pain; Castiglione wrote to the Marchioness, his mother, "I am at Rome, but seem no longer there, since my poor Raffaelle is gone."

Rome, in the eyes of the most spiritual writer of the time, had lost its chief charm and ornament: "If grief be in proportion to the loss sustained, no loss of this kind could cause a grief equal to that occasioned by the death of Raffaelle; who, having gained the highest reputation for his works which genius can give, was cut off at an age, which, with most men, is yet only that of hope."

Raffaelle's body lay in state in his own house, according to the custom of the time and country. The apartment where it lay, was that in which still hung suspended on the scaffolding which supported it, the picture of The Transfiguration, finished, but still perhaps wanting in some parts a

his person and manner of living, and in the taste of his works, the most striking contrast to Raffaelle. Every time Raffaelle went to court, he had a train of fifty painters, all of them notable artists, who attended to do him honor. Michel Angelo said to Raffaelle one day as the latter passed by his house, 'You march with a grand retinue, like a General!' 'And you,' replied Raffaelle, 'go alone, like a hangman.'"

last touch; in the language of Pliny, "the spectator seems to behold the pencil of the artist fall from his dying hand in the midst of his work."

An immense cortege of friends, pupils, artists, celebrated writers, personages of every rank, accompanied the body to the Pantheon, where it was deposited, amidst the lamentations of the whole city of Rome.

It will be seen from the character of Raffaelle, that irritability and morbid sensibility are not, as many suppose, the inevitable concomitants of genius. They are *diseases* of noble minds. The young artist *aims* at perfection, but he may not be disheartened because he cannot attain to it. Self-respect should prevent extreme anxiety about the opinion of the world at large; a fair estimate of his own abilities, nerve him to encounter criticism, just and unjust. Youthful aspirants for fame, occasionally haunt the exhibition room to listen to the remarks of careless spectators. The old proverb, for such cases made and provided, too frequently holds true, and they go away with a rankling "thorn in the side."

These critics many times are like the one whom the ancient sculptor reproved, with—"Cobler, stick to your shoe"*— and know as little of art as did that pretensious sandal maker; yet as they have the power to wound, they should be carefully shunned. A craving for the gratification of vanity, should be conquered at once, or it will fret away the very life of the artist.

*Ne sutor ultra crepidam.

He wishes to succeed—may he not listen to the whisperings of Hope? May he not drink in with delight the praises that sound sweetly to his ear? He wishes to succeed! The talent of success is nothing more than doing what you can do well; and *doing well whatever you do;* without a thought of fame. If it come at all, it will come because it is deserved, not because it is sought after. The artist lives so much in a world of his own, as to be in danger of forgetting that he still belongs to a common-place world, where common-place people abound, who have no *better* than common-sense. These good people are not to be despised. He cannot live without them, but they may live without him. They form the foundation and solid walls of society—he is only ornamental; both are useful. The giant tree cannot say to the tiny flower upon its waving branches, "I have no need of thee;" the flower cannot say to the rugged roots, "I have no need of thee." Too frequently the artist alienates himself from his fellow-men, because he has no sympathy with their every-day pursuits. This is all wrong. The artist should be, as Goethe hath it, "a many-sided man," capable of entering cordially into the multifarious interests of humanity, and a large-hearted man, responding sympathetically to all its joys and griefs. He is not, like an oyster, to shut himself up

"In a choice shell of pride;"

no "island," severed from the continent of social life, but part and parcel of that life. He should be a genial part of it, too, and shed the light of loving-kindness along his every-day pathway.

The artist must beware of becoming a *visionary;* a *castle-builder;* a *day-dreamer.* Alas, how many hours, nay years, have been wasted by the sons of genius, in mere musing upon what they might, could, would, or should do, instead of doing it. "My mind makes pictures when my eyes are shut," said Wordsworth; and these day-dreamers prefer making pictures in the same way, while the canvas stands neglected on the easel, or the marble remains a shapeless block. Reverie becomes a habit of mind as difficult to overcome as opium-eating, and the fantastic shapes which people the brain of the day-dreaming artist are of no more use to the world, than the wild ravings of the opium-eater.

The "baseless fabrics" of the visionary, are to be clearly distinguished from the conceptions which take shape and beauty in the mind of the artist, and which bide their time, to become visible in palpable forms.

In the solitude of the studio, there is great temptation to fall into those delicious musings, which "lap the soul in Elysium," yet leave it vapid, listless, inert.

These artists "never are, but always to be," super-excellent. Their castles reach to the third heaven; but float away with the passing cloud. They despise the dull plodder who acts up to the painter's maxim—*nulla dies sine linea;* weeks and months pass without a line from them, while every stroke of the steady pencil marks sure progress in excellence.

This indulgence in visionary delight became a positive mania with the English painter, Blake, and a sketch of his life may furnish a striking and useful lesson to the young artist. William Blake,* at the early age of ten, was an artist, and at twelve wrote poetry. From that age till thirty he wrote some really good verses, but many of them were wild and incoherent, and in them may be traced "the dawning of those strange, mystical and mysterious fancies, in which he subsequently misemployed his pencil."

He learned the art of engraving with a good master, and was, besides, the occasional pupil of Flaxman and Fuseli.

What was very remarkable about Blake, was his daily industry. He seemed to live two distinct lives. During the day he worked industriously with the graver; but when night came he gave himself up to seeing visions and writing mad poetry. At the age of six and twenty, Blake married the "dark eyed Kate," of several of his lyric poems.

She proved one of the most devoted of wives, yet she did not aid him, in the least, to conquer his visionary propensities, or impart to him an iota of common sense. "She believed him to be the finest genius on earth; she believed in his verse; she believed in his designs; and to the wildest flights of his imagination she bowed the knee, and was a worshiper."

* Born in London, 1757.

However, she had herself some practical domestic virtues, and although she indulged him in his absurdities, was a prudent, frugal wife. "She found out the way of being happy at home, living on the simplest of food, and contented in the homeliest of clothing. She whom Blake emphatically called his 'beloved,' was no ordinary woman. She wrought off the impressions of his plates; she colored them with a light and neat hand, and made drawings much in the spirit of her husband's composition." But Katharine Blake saw no visions. She worked and toiled, kept shop, when her husband set up as a print-seller, and when he proved unsuccessful in speculations and experiments, she soothed and encouraged him. He wrote songs, composed music, and when he was in the humor, used the pencil and the graver.

His "Songs of Innocence and Experience" are original and natural. The paintings illustrate the verse, and are curiously mingled with it. The designs, however, have been said to be, "more allied to heaven than to earth—a kind of spiritual abstractions."

As a specimen of his poetry, the following lines are given accompanying his picture of Innocence:—

Piping down the valleys wild,
  Piping songs of pleasant glee,
On a cloud I saw a child,
  And he, laughing, said to me—

Pipe a song about a lamb;
  So I piped with merry cheer.

Piper, pipe that song again;
  So I piped—he wept to hear.

Drop thy pipe, thy happy pipe,
  Sing thy songs of happy cheer;
So I sang the same again,
  While he wept with joy to hear.

Piper, sit thee down and write
  In a book that all may read;
So he vanished from my sight,
  And I plucked a hollow reed,

And I made a rural pen,
  And I stained the water clear;
And I wrote my happy songs,
  Every child may joy to hear.

His designs were even more difficult to understand than his poems. His imaginary visitations, or visions, furnished the themes. He engraved both the poetry and the figures on copper, and afterwards tinted them in a peculiar manner. There was much beauty in the designs, though the meaning was obscure.

His mind could convert the most ordinary occurrences into something supernatural.

"Did you ever see a fairy's funeral?" said he to a lady who happened to sit by him in company.

"Never, sir," was the answer.

"I have," said Blake; "but not before last night. I was walking alone in my garden; there was great stillness among the branches and flowers, and more than common sweetness in the air; I heard a low and pleasant sound, and

15

I knew not whence it came. At last I saw the broad leaf of a flower move, and underneath I saw a procession of creatures of the size and color of green and gray grasshoppers, bearing a body laid out on a rose leaf, which they buried with songs, and then disappeared. It was a fairy funeral."

On another occasion, a gentleman, a friend of Blake, took from a private drawer a small panel, on which was a painting, and showed it to another gentleman to whom he had been exhibiting a number of the artist's drawings from visionary persons, who had condescended to sit to him. "This is the last which I shall show you," said he; "but it is the greatest curiosity of all. Only look at the splendor of the coloring, and the original character of the thing."

"I see," replied the other, "a naked figure, with a strong body and a short neck, with burning eyes which long for moisture, and a face worthy of a murderer, holding a bloody cup in its clawed hands, but of which it seems eager to drink. I never saw any shape so strange, nor did I ever see any coloring so curiously splendid; a kind of glistening green and dusky gold, beautifully varnished. But what in the world is it?"

"It is a ghost, sir—the ghost of a flea—a spiritualization of the thing."

"You saw this in a vision, then?"

"I'll tell you all about it, sir. I called one evening on Blake and found him more than usually excited. He told me he had seen a wonderful thing—the ghost of a flea. 'And did you make a drawing of him,' I enquired. 'No indeed,' said he, 'I wish I had; but I shall if he appears again.' He looked earnestly into a corner of the room, and then said: 'Here he is—reach me my things—I shall keep my eye on him. There he comes, his eager tongue whisking out of his mouth, a cup in his hand to hold blood, and covered with a scaly skin of gold and green.' As he described him so he drew him."

Another friend called one evening on Blake and found him sitting with a pencil and panel, drawing a portrait with all the seeming anxiety of a man who is conscious that he has got a fastidious sitter; he looked and drew, and drew and looked, yet no living being was visible.

"Disturb me not," said Blake in a whisper; "I have one sitting to me."

"Sitting to you!" exclaimed the astonished visitor; "where is he, and what is he? I see none."

"But I see him, sir," answered Blake haughtily; "there he is; his name is Lot. You may read of him in the Scriptures. He is sitting for his portrait."

Even when he was indulging in these laughable fancies, and seeing visions at the request of his friends, he conceived and engraved a series of illustrations of the Book of Job, which have been acknowledged as "simple and sublime."

Poor Blake drew and engraved this series in a small

room—his kitchen, parlor, bedroom, and studio—with the faithful Katharine for his only companion. Indeed, he seldom saw company—real flesh and blood company—but lived in the midst of London like a hermit,

"With one fair spirit for his minister."

His income at this time did not amount to more than seventeen or eighteen shillings a week.

He continued to execute these singular productions, enduring a life of labor and privation, until he was in his seventy-first year. Old age came upon him and found him feeble and in want. Still he saw visions, and attempted to fix them upon canvas.

Three days before his death, he sat bolstered up in bed and tinted one of his favorite pictures in his happiest style. He touched, and retouched it—held it at arms length, and then threw it from him, exclaiming, "There, that will do! I cannot mend it."

He saw his wife in tears; she felt that this was to be the last of his works. "Stay, Kate!" cried Blake, "keep just as you are—I will draw your portrait—for you have ever been an angel to me." She obeyed, and the dying artist made a fine likeness.

"Blake was a poet, a *dreamer* and an *enthusiast.* The eminence which it had been the first ambition of his youth to climb, was visible before him; and he saw on its ascent, or on its summit, those who had started earlier in the race.

He felt conscious of his own merit, and thought he had only to sing songs and draw designs, to become great and famous. The crosses which genius is heir to had been wholly unforeseen, and they befel him early.

"His works are looked coldly on by the world, and were only esteemed by men of poetic minds, or those who were fond of things out of the common way."

By frequent indulgence in wild romantic imaginings, "he gradually began to believe in the reality of what dreaming fancy painted, and the pictured forms which swarmed before his eyes, assumed, in his apprehension, the stability and truth of positive revelations; he mistook the vivid figures for the poets, heroes and princes of old. He conceived that he had formed friendships with Homer and Moses, with Pindar and Virgil, with Dante and Milton.

"Of the existence of Blake" says Allan Cunningham, "few men of taste could be ignorant; of his great merits multitudes knew, nor was his extreme poverty any secret. Yet he, one of the ornaments of the age, was reduced to a miserable garret and a crust of bread, and would have perished from want, had not some friends, neither wealthy nor powerful, averted this disgrace from coming upon our country."

## CHAPTER XX.

### HIGH AIMS.

"And for success, I ask no more than this,—
To bear unflinching witness to the truth.
All true whole men succeed; for what is worth
Success' name, unless it be the thought,
The inward surety, to have carried out
A noble purpose to a noble end!"—*Lowell.*

THE dangers and difficulties which beset like fiery dragons the road to *eminence* in Art, might seem sufficient to deter the most adventurous artist-errant from the pursuit. And they *should* deter all who are not conscious of possessing the skill and the strength to overcome them. It is no easy path of joyous dalliance even to the most gifted—it is the path to certain destruction to such as enter it merely because they think it an easy and honorable highway for all who choose to walk in it. But to drop the meagre metaphor; the young man who takes up the pallet or the chisel to escape from the counter, the desk, the college, or the farm, and expects in that way to better his condition will find himself grievously disappointed.

An earnest, unconquerable love of art, for its own sake, ought to be, in every instance, the main cause for adopting the trials and labors of the artist. It is not an El Dorado nor a fairy land, nor to be won by a single blow; but by line upon line, stroke upon stroke,* day after day, and night after night, through long years of patient labor. Yet Art, to its true votaries, is, what Coleridge said poetry had been to him, "its own exceeding great reward."

The artist's aim is to exhibit truth and beauty. "The one condition coupled with the gift of truth, is its use." The mathematician, after reading Milton's Paradise Lost, could ask, "what does it prove?" and many a cold-hearted and dull-witted man has said of painting and poetry—"what is their use?" Painting and sculpture, are a visible language, which conveys thoughts more vividly than any other language, not excepting poetry itself. "Nature is a revelation of God; art is a revelation of man."

The artist, in our country, must do what lies clearly at hand. That may be only to paint portraits. Even so; let him not despise the day of small things. "Knowest thou *yesterday*, its aim and reason? Workest thou well *to-day* for *worthy things?* Then calmly wait the *morrow's* hidden season. And fear not thou, what hap soe'er it brings!" It is true, that the portraits of the greater portion of mankind, are without interest, excepting to a very limited circle. But to that limited circle, they are inexpressibly valuable; and

* "What tedious training, year after year, never ending, to form the common sense; what continual reproduction of annoyances, inconveniences, dilemmas, what *rejoicings over us of little men;* what disputing of prices, what reckonings of interest; and all to form the hand to the mind, to instruct us that *good thoughts are no better than good dreams unless they be executed.*

the artist who ministers thus to domestic and social affection, has done a *worthy* work.

Ambition may prompt to higher efforts, and genius sigh for an opportunity to exercise itself on more congenial subjects. In our country, the sculptor and the painter are called upon by public bodies, for the portraits of our good and great men. Such portraits are, to all intents and purposes, *historical.* They are the very bones and sinews of our future history. They are to look down from the halls of justice and legislation, the college and academy, upon the old and the young of coming generations, inspiring them with heroism, patriotism and virtue.

These "labors of love" will prepare the artist for that more etherial region of Parnassus, to which he constantly aspires.

He has a lofty aim. He proudly says, "I am living for eternity." Be it so. Let each, and all, follow out the leading of their idiosyncracy in art, and be just what nature intended. If they do not, no matter what the "motives" may be, to which they devote time and thought, their works will become puerile, artificial, affected, and inefficient.

They have received a gift from God, which they must render back—the five or ten talents—with generous interest.

"We can conceive of some village Michel Angelo, with a soul too mighty for its tenement of clay, whose longing aspirations after truth and good were palsied by the refusal of his hand to execute them, struggling to burst the trammels and trying to shake off the load of discouragement that oppressed him. What must be his exultation, to see the speaking statue, the stately pile, rise up slowly before him; the idea in his mind embodied out of nothing, without model or precedent—to see a huge cathedral heave its ponderous weight above the earth, or the solemn figure of an apostle point from one corner of it to the skies; and to think that future ages would perhaps gaze at the work with the same delight and wonder that his own did, and not suffer his name to sink into the same oblivion as those who had gone before him, or as the brutes to perish; this was, indeed, to be admitted into the communion of genius."

"The field lies wide before you, where to reap
The noble harvest of a deathless name."

strong personal enthusiasm, a vivid sense of the facts which come before her, and a clear ready method of narration. 'The Mechanic' is a volume in the right vein, neither dry nor didactic, but with a few spirited words at the outset, leading the young reader to facts of warning and encouragement in the lives of distinguished Americans. A good book for country circulation and common school libraries."—*Literary World.*

"No better books can be found for family instruction, and they should be in every Lyceum and District School Library of the country."—*Newark Eagle*

"An excellent book, by a talented and popular authoress. It is designed for the laudable and wise end of enlightening, interesting and urging onward, in the paths of prosperity and science, the young man. And it abounds in extraordinary instances of perseverance, peculiar branches of study adopted, plans pursued, with appropriate essays, valuable hints upon character, and the like. Its contents are varied, and its biographical notes add much to its general interest."—*Fredonian.*

"Full of excellent advice, practical suggestions, and interesting notices. The biographical sketches are admirable."—*Savannah Republican.*

"An excellent little book, and we are persuaded it makes out the sure path to complete success. It is a great lesson to teach the young that the elements of success are within themselves. That lesson Mrs. Tuthill enforces, and expatiates upon it in a manner fitted to fix it in the mind of the reader."—*Oneida Herald.*

---

## GENERAL LANE'S BRIGADE IN MEXICO.

BY A. G. BRACKETT, M. D.

---

## PIONEER HISTORY.

Being an Account of the First Examinations of the Ohio Valley, and the Early Settlement of the Northwest Territory. By S. P. Hildreth.

---

## PIONEER SETTLERS OF OHIO.

Biographical and Historical Memoirs of the Early Pioneer Settlers of Ohio, with Narratives of Incidents and Occurrences in 1775. By S. P. Hildreth.

---

## GRIMKE ON FREE INSTITUTIONS.

Considerations upon the Nature and Tendency of Free Institutions. By Frederick Grimke.

## LAYARD'S NINEVEH.

A Popular Account of Discoveries at Nineveh. By Austen Henry Layard. With Numerous Engravings.

## THE LIFE OF FRANCIS MARION.

BY WILLIAM GILMORE SIMMS. ENGRAVINGS.

## HILLS, LAKES, AND FOREST STREAMS;

or, A Tramp in the Chateaugay Woods. By S. H. Hammond.

## MORNING STARS OF THE NEW WORLD.

Christopher Columbus—Americus Vespucius—Ferdinand de Soto—Sir Walter Raleigh—Henry Hudson—Capt. John Smith—Capt. Miles Standish—Lady Arabella Johnson—John Eliot—Wm. Penn. By H. F. Parker. Engravings.

**The Life and Letters of Stephen Olin, D. D., LL. D. 2 vols.**

## GREECE AND THE GOLDEN HORN.

By Rev. Dr. Olin. Edited by Rev. Dr. McClintock.

## SCHOOL ARCHITECTURE;

or, Contributions to the Improvement of School Houses in the United States. By Henry Barnard, LL. D.

This volume of 464 pages, is an enlarged and improved edition of a work, which was pronounced by a Committee of the American Association for the Advancement of Education, of which Prof. Henry, of the Smithsonian Institution was Chairman, "the most thorough, scientific and practical description of the subject which has appeared in this country, or in Europe." It contains:

1. An exposition, from official documents, of common errors in the location, construction and furniture of school-houses, as they have been heretofore almost universally built, even in States where the subject of Education has received the most attention.

2. A discussion of the purposes to be answered, and the principles to be observed in structures designed for schools.

3. Plans, with minute descriptions and specifications, adapted to schools of every grade and size, in a variety of styles, and on a large or small scale of expense, either recommended by experienced educators, or followed in buildings recently erected.

4. Numerous illustrations of the most approved modes of constructing and arranging seats and desks, and of all recent improvements for warming and ventilating school-rooms and public halls generally.

5. Catalogues of maps, globes, and other means of visible illustration and practical experiments, with which each grade of schools should be furnished.

6. A list of books on Education, Schools and School Systems, and of books of reference, for the use of Teachers and the older scholars of every school.

7. Rules and Regulations for the care and preservation of School-houses, Grounds and Furniture.

8. Example of Exercises suitable to the dedication of School-houses.

9. A variety of Hints respecting the Classification of Schools.

This work has been strongly recommended by the most eminent educators, teachers, and school officials, and has been distributed among School Districts by the Legislatures of Ohio, Connecticut, Rhode Island, Massachusetts, Vermont, and New Hampshire. It has already wrought a revolution in the construction, ventilation and furniture of school-houses in many parts of the country.

---

## LOSSING'S LIVES OF THE SIGNERS.

Biographical Sketches of the Signers of the Declaration of American Independence; the Declaration Historically Considered; and a Sketch of the Leading Events connected with the Adoption of the Articles of Confederation, and of the Federal Constitution. By B. J. Lossing. 50 Engravings.

---

## HOWE'S EMINENT MECHANICS.

Memoirs of the most Eminent American Mechanics; also, Lives of Distinguished European Mechanics; together with a Collection of Anecdotes, Descriptions, etc., relating to the Mechanic Arts. By Henry Howe. With 50 Engravings.

**First Series.**

The Swiss Family Robinson;
or, Adventures of a Father, Mother, and Four Sons, on a Desert Island. Engravings. 2 vols.

Adventures of Daniel Boone,
the Kentucky Rifleman. By the author of "Uncle Philip."

Abbott's History of Maria Antoinette.
Engravings.

The Young Sailor.
A Narrative founded on Fact. By Mary S. B. Dana.

Sandford and Merton.
By Thomas Day.

Conquest and Self-Conquest;
or, Which is the Hero? By Miss Mackintosh.

Boyhood of Great Men;
Intended as an Example for Youth. Engravings.

Abbott's History of Madame Roland.
Engravings.

Abbott's History of Alexander the Great.
Engravings.

Live and Let Live;
or, Domestic Service Illustrated. By Miss C. M. Sedgwick.

Benjamin Franklin:
His Autobiography, continued by Rev. H. H. Weld. Copiously illustrated.

Lives of the Signers of the Declaration of Independence.
By Benson J. Lossing.

Howe's Mechanics.
Lives of Eminent American and European Mechanics. By Henry Howe. 50 engravings.

Hallam's Middle Ages.
View of the State of Europe during the Middle Ages. By Henry Hallam.

Two Years Before the Mast;
a Personal Narrative of Life at Sea. By R. H. Dana, Jr.

The Pursuit of Knowledge under Difficulties;
its Pleasures and Rewards; illustrated by Memoirs of Eminent Men. By Geo. L. Craik. 2 vols.

Russia as it is.
By Count A. de Gurowski.

Letters to Young Ladies.
By Mrs. L. H. Sigourney.

Layard's Nineveh.
A popular Account of Discoveries at Nineveh. Engravings.

Curran and his Contemporaries.
By Charles Phillips.

Life of Sir Isaac Newton.
By Sir David Brewster. Engravings.

Lives of Celebrated Female Sovereigns.
By Mrs. Jameson. 2 vols.

Life of Francis Marion.
By William G. Simms. Engravings.

The Merchant.
Illustrative of Success in Life. By Mrs. Louisa C. Tuthill.

The Sketch-Book.
By Washington Irving.

Life of General Lafayette.
By William Cutter. Portrait.

Taylor's History of Ohio,
to the Organization of the Northwest T..ritory, in 1787.

## Second Series.

Adventures of Hernan Cortez, Conqueror of Mexico.
By "Uncle Philip."

History of England.
By Charles Dickens. 2 vols.

History of Hannibal,
the Carthaginian. By Jacob Abbott. Engravings

Moral Tales.
By Maria Edgeworth. 2 vols.

Rodolphus;
a Franconia Story. By Jacob Abbott. Engravings

The Vicar of Wakefield.
By Oliver Goldsmith.

The Sunshine of Greystone;
a Story for Girls. By E. J. May. Engravings.

The Crofton Boys;
a Tale for Youth. By Harriet Martineau.

Masterman Ready;
or, the Wreck of the Pacific. By Capt. Francis Marryat.

Life of Washington.
By Jared Sparks.

Dr. Smith's History of Greece.
From the Earliest Times to the Roman Conquest. Edited by Prof. Geo. W. Greene. Engravings.

Tytler's Universal History.
From the Creation of the World to the Decease of George III. 6 vols.

Ranke's Civil Wars and Monarchy in France,
in the 16th and 17th Centuries; a History of France principally during that period.

Hildreth's Theory of Politics:
an Inquiry into the Foundations of Governments, and the Causes and Progress of Political Revolutions.

Elements of Geology.
By Professors Alonzo Gray, and C. B. Adams.

Life and Letters of Barthold George Niebuhr.
By the Chevalier Bunsen.

Life of Nelson.
By Robert Southey.

Richardson's Arctic Searching Expedition;
a Journal of a Boat-Voyage through Rupert's Land and the Arctic Sea, in Search of Sir John Franklin.

Life and Travels of Mungo Park.

The Lawyer.
By Louisa C. Tuthill.

Pioneer Settlers of Ohio.
Biographical and Historical Memoirs of the Early Pioneer Settlers of Ohio, with Narratives of Incidents and Occurrences in 1775. By S. P. Hildreth, M. D.

Monasteries of the East;
embracing Visits to Monasteries on the Levant. By Curzon.

Marco Paul's Travels and Adventures.
City of New York. By Jacob Abbott.

**Third Series.**

Adventures of Captain John Smith,
the Founder of the Colony of Virginia. By the author of "Uncle Philip."

Abbott's History of Queen Elizabeth.
Engravings.

Frank.
By Maria Edgeworth. 2 vols.

Ellen Linn;
a Franconia Story. By Jacob Abbott. Engravings.

Adventures of Robinson Crusoe.
By Daniel Defoe. Engravings.

Abbott's History of Julius Cæsar.
Engravings.

Never too Late.
By Charles Burdett.

The Son of a Genius.
By Mrs. Hofland.

Plutarch's Lives;
translated by Langhorne. 4 vols.

Creasy's Decisive Battles.
The Fifteen Decisive Battles of the World. By E. S. Creasy.

Life of Christopher Columbus.
By Washington Irving.

Abbott's History of Cyrus the Great.
Engravings.

Farm Implements,
and the Principles of their Construction and Use; an Elementary and Familiar Treatise on Mechanics, and on Natural Philosophy generally, as applied to Agriculture. By Jno. G. Thomas. 200 Illustrations.

Stephens' Incidents of Travel
in Greece, Turkey, Russia, and Poland. 2 vols.

Lives of the Brothers Humboldt,
Alexander and William; translated from the German, by Juliette Bauer.

Glimpses of Spain.
By S. T. Wallis.

Nile Notes
of a Howadji. By G. W. Curtis.

Thatcher's Indian Traits;
being Sketches of the Manners, Customs, and Characters of the North American Natives.

Circumnavigation of the Globe;
an Historical Account of the Progress of Discovery in the Pacific Ocean, from the Voyage of Magellan to the Death of Cook.

James' History of Chivalry and the Crusades.

The Whale and his Captors;
or, Whalemen's Adventures and the Whale's Biography. By Rev. H. T. Cheever.

The Mechanic.
By Mrs. Louisa C. Tuthill.

Alice Franklin.
By Mary Howitt.

The Young Man's Book;
or, Self-Education. By William Hosmer.

## Fourth Series.

The Adventures of Henry Hudson;
By the author of "Uncle Philip."

Abbott's History of the Empress Josephine.
Engravings.

Harry and Lucy.
By Maria Edgeworth. 2 vols.

Praise and Principle;
or, For Which Shall I Live? By Miss Maria J. McIntosh.

Edgar Clifton;
or, Right and Wrong. By C. Adams. Engravings.

Uncle Philip's Whale Fishery.
Conversations with the Children about the Whale Fishery and the Polar Seas. 2 vols.

Abbott's History of Alfred the Great.
Engravings.

Hope on, Hope ever!
By Mary Howitt.

Dr. Smith's History of Rome.
Engravings.

Robertson's America.
History of the Discovery and Settlement of America.

Abbott's History of Mary Queen of Scots.
Engravings.

Story of the Peninsular War.
By the Marquis of Londonderry.

Hume's History of England.
6 vols.

Gerstaecker's Narrative
of a Journey Round the World.

A Lady's Voyage Round the World.
By Madame Ida Pfeiffer.

Lives of Distinguished Females.

The Court and Camp of Bonaparte.
Being Sketches of his Family, Ministers, Marshals, etc.

History of Wonderful Inventions.
Illustrated.

Taylor's History of Ireland.
2 vols.

The Use of the Body in Relation to the Mind.
By Dr. George Moore.

The Illustrated Natural History.
By Rev. J. G. Wood. 450 engravings.

Dew's Ancient and Modern Nations.
The Laws, Customs, Manners and Institutions of the Ancient and Modern Nations. By Thomas Dew.

**Supplementary Series.**

Barnard's School Architecture;
embracing the Principles to be observed in the erection of School-Houses; Ventilation and Warming; School Furniture and Apparatus; with numerous Plans and Illustrations.

Bancroft's United States.
History of the United States, from the Discovery of the American Continent. By George Bancroft. 5 vols.

Lossing's Pictorial Revolution.
The Pictorial Field Book of the Revolution; or, Illustrations, by Pen and Pencil, of the History, Biography, Scenery, Relics, and Traditions of the War for Independence. By Benson J. Lossing. With several hundred engravings on wood, by Lossing and Barritt, chiefly from original sketches by the author. 2 vols.

Prescott's Mexico.
History of the Conquest of Mexico, with a Preliminary View of the Ancient Mexican Civilization, and the Life of the Conqueror, Hernando Cortez. By William H. Prescott. 3 vols.

The Grinnell Expedition.
The U. S. Grinnell Expedition in Search of Sir John Franklin. A Personal Narrative. By Elisha Kent Kane, M. D., U. S. N. With numerous illustrations.

Select British Eloquence;
embracing the best Speeches Entire, of the most Eminent Orators of Great Britain, for the last two Centuries; with Sketches of

their Lives, an Estimate of their Genius, and Notes, Critical and Explanatory. By Chauncey A. Goodrich, D. D.

Thiers' French Revolution.

The History of the French Revolution. By M. A. Thiers, late Prime Minister of France. Translated, with Notes and Illustrations from the most Authentic Sources, by Frederick Shoberl. 4 vols.

The Poets and Poetry of Europe.

With Introductions and Biographical Notices. By Henry Wadsworth Longfellow.

Prose Writers of Germany.

By Frederic H. Hedge. With portraits.

The Poets and Poetry of America,

to the Middle of the Nineteenth Century. By Rufus W. Griswold.

The Prose Writers of America.

With a Survey of the Intellectual History, Condition, and Prospects of the Country. By Rufus W. Griswold.

Lynch's Dead Sea Expedition.

Narrative of the Dead Sea Expedition. By Captain Lynch.

Morning Stars of the New World.

Christopher Columbus—Americus Vespucius—Ferdinand de Soto—Sir Walter Raleigh—Henry Hudson—Capt. John Smith—Captain Miles Standish—Lady Arabella Johnson—John Eliot—William Penn. By H. F. Parker.

Washington and his Generals.

George Washington—Major Generals Putnam, Montgomery, Arnold, Stark, Schuyler, Gates, Steuben, Wayne, Conway, Mifflin, Ward, Heath, Greene, Moultrie, Knox, Lincoln, Lee, Clinton, Sullivan, St. Clair, Marion, Stirling, La Fayette, De Kalb, and others. By J. T. Headley. 2 vols.

Life of Patrick Henry.

By William Wirt.

Pencillings by the Way:

Written during some years of Residence and Travel in Europe. By N. Parker Willis.

Summer Cruise in the Mediterranean,

on board an American Frigate. By N. Parker Willis.

## Guizot's History of Civilization.

The History of Civilization, from the Fall of the Roman Empire to the French Revolution. By F. Guizot. Translated by W. Hazlitt. 4 vols.

## Gibbon's Rome.

The Decline and Fall of the Roman Empire. By Edward Gibbon. 6 vols.

## Physical Geography.

By Mary Somerville. With Notes, etc., by W. S. W. Ruschenberger, M. D.

## Lives of the Queens of England,

from the Norman Conquest; with Anecdotes of their Courts. By Agnes Strickland. 6 vols.

## Wilkinson's Ancient Egyptians.

A Popular Account of the Ancient Egyptians. By Sir J. Gardner Wilkinson. 500 Engravings. 2 vols.

## Astoria;

or, Anecdotes of an Enterprise beyond the Rocky Mountains. By Washington Irving.

## Pictorial History of England.

Being a History of the People as well as of the Kingdom. 4 vols.

## Bayard Taylor's Africa.

A Journey to Central Africa; or, Life and Landscapes from Egypt to the Negro Kingdoms of the White Nile. By Bayard Taylor.

## The Mexican War:

a History of its Origin, and a Detailed Account of the Victories which terminated in the Surrender of the Capital. By Edward D. Mansfield.

## Legends of the West.

By James Hall.

## An Art-Student in Munich.

By Anna Mary Howitt.

## Six Months in Italy.

By George S. Hillard.

## The Earth and Man:

Lectures on Comparative Physical Geography, in its Relation to the History of Mankind. By Arnold Guyot.

Headley's War of 1812.
The History of the Second War with Great Britain. By J. T. Headley. 2 vols.

The Women of the Revolution.
By Mrs. E. F. Ellet. 3 vols.

Pioneer Women of the West.
By Mrs. E. F. Ellet.

Home Life in Germany.
By C. L. Brace.

Chambers' Miscellany
of Useful and Entertaining Knowledge. Edited by Wm. Chambers. 10 vols.

Longfellow's Poems.
Poems, by Henry Wadsworth Longfellow. 2 vols.

Dana's Poems.
Poems, by Richard Henry Dana.

Bryant's Poems.
Poems, by William Cullen Bryant.

Lectures on the Progress of Arts and Sciences,
resulting from the Great Exhibition in London, delivered by Professors Whewell, De la Beche, Owen, Bell, Playfair, Lindley, Solly, Willis, Glaisher, Hensman, Royle, and Washington.

Greece and the Golden Horn.
By Rev. Stephen Olin, D. D.

Twenty Years in the Philippines.
By Paul P. de la Gironière. With Illustrations.

Stephens' Central America.
Incidents of Travel in Central America, Chiapas, and Yucatan 2 vols.

A Winter in Madeira:
and a Summer in Spain and Florence. By John A. Dix.

Johnson's Works.
The Works of Samuel Johnson, LL. D. 2 vols.

The Behavior Book:
A Manual for Ladies. By Miss Leslie.

www.ingramcontent.com/pod-product-compliance
Lightning Source LLC
LaVergne TN
LVHW050534100826
845148LV00002B/552

* 9 7 8 1 4 2 5 5 8 4 6 8 9 *